The South has a long tradition of fine storytellers, and now a new one comes along, perhaps better than all the rest. Jim Ritchie isn't bashful; he jumps right in, holding the reader spellbound with his uproariously earthy frankness. A master teller in the oral tradition, the author performs even better on the stage of these pages, making his subjects come to life with his own homespun style.

SHOCCO TALES is at once humorous, yet loving. It's kind of like a raw oyster: rough on the outside, delicious on the inside, yet even better flavored with the South's ubiquitous peppery seasoning. And Jim Ritchie has had plenty of peppery experiences; more than most folks could cram into several lifetimes, perhaps.

The reader who has grown up in the South will swear that he knows each and every character in these tales: from the "Indian doctor" with the secret hemorrhoid cure to the bull who couldn't keep his "loins" out of reach of the youngster's BB gun; he'll identify with Bubba gigging for Giant Southern Frogs and with the curious cat that burnt the cabin down; he'll remember high school teammates like "Shorty," and "Speedy," as well as college fraternity brothers like "Snake" and "Stud." And he'll laugh while remembering.

The reader who came of age elsewhere will soon know what he missed, and to rectify that, will immediately begin a quest for real estate somewhere close to Shocco, Mississippi.

Shocco Tales:
Southern Fried Sagas

Best Wishes

Jim Hitchie

Shocco Tales:
Southern Fried Sagas

by

Jim Ritchie

with artwork by

Perry Thickens Ritchie

Shocco Stories   Canton, Mississippi

Library of Congress Cataloging-in-Publication Data
     (Pending)

Shocco Stories
P. O. Box 235
Canton, Mississippi 39046

ISBN 0-9656002-0-3 (previously ISBN 1-879034-07-7)

Second printing, 1997

DEDICATION

To Helen Perry Thickens Ritchie:

Wife,
Mother,
Artist,
Helpmate,
Confidant,
Tolerator of bird dogs and muddy boots;

I'm a blessed man.

TABLE OF CONTENTS

ACKNOWLEDGEMENTS

Where do I start? So much encouragement and help from so many good people. Gin McElwee and Sandra Baggett for linking me up with Bob and Betsy Neill. Bob and Betsy, of course, for all the advice and pep rallies. Kent Stocker for risking his expensive camera equipment to take pictures of me. Perry for suggesting the whole thing to start with and using her incredible gifts of art to illustrate this book. And to the many other friends who've read the manuscripts and furthered the cause by offering their advice, laughter, and, some unwittingly at the time, by playing leading roles in most of these stories and those stories to come. Thanks, guys.

INTRODUCTION

Let's me and you clear up something right up front. I ain't a writer by trade and this ain't a book on religion. Now that my conscience is clear on that and before you decide to take this thing home, you need to understand what I've done here.

That I ain't a writer should be painfully apparent even by now, but I've always liked to tell stories. Matter of fact, I'd rather tell a joke or story than eat chocolate ice cream, and I do love chocolate ice cream.

My bride of many years sat me down one day not too long ago and pinned me with those clear blue eyes of hers.

"You ought to write some of these stories down," she said.

So I did the only thing a hairy-chested, testosterone-filled, macho husband could do. I said, "Yes ma'am," got me a yellow pad, licked the point of a pencil, and had at it.

I've been asked if writing them down is harder than telling them. That's a fair question I reckon, but the answer is no. (Well, maybe a little harder, since I have to look up spelling sometimes. "Testosterone" was looked up, for example, because it didn't just jump right out at me.) I wrote 'em like I tell 'em.

And that's what this book is. A random bunch of tales and musings and remembrances, some more important than others, but nothing truly earth shattering. No advice on saving time or making money or improving memory or losing weight, since I've never done any of those things. A sort of a breather from that stuff, really.

I may have stretched the truth a smidgen in some of the stories. And you'll find out if you read this book that I've done some things I'm going to have to answer for in the hereafter. I have, however, cleaned up my act considerably as my hairline has receded and my waistline expanded, but there's still room for a whole lot of improvement.

Nevertheless, I think that God might look down at me and grin and shake His head and sigh and overlook some of it. I sure as hell hope He does.

Shocco Tales:
Southern Fried Sagas

COUNTRY BOY

I live at Shocco, Mississippi. It's amazing to me how many folks don't seem to know where Shocco is. I can go to Chicago or Miami or someplace like that and when the inevitable question of where I'm from is asked and I tell them Shocco, Mississippi, they look at me like I just blew in from Jupiter. They generally got just as much idea where Shocco is as where Jupiter is. Then I clear it up for them when I tell them that it really ain't hard to find. You just draw a line from Sharon, Mississippi to Ratliff Ferry, Mississippi, and Shocco falls pretty near right on the line, shading just a little bit toward Ratliff Ferry. They almost always nod and change the subject. So I reckon that clears up the location for them. I hope it has for you, in case you don't know your geography too good, either.

Ratliff Ferry Road runs right in front of my house, and we don't have much traffic. The cars or trucks or tractors that do come by usually have somebody we know in them or on them, so we exchange waves, if I'm in the front yard. The strangers who ride by must be glad to see some form of civilization, because they wave, too. The house sits far enough back off the road that they can't see anybody in my back yard. Which makes it a lot easier on me when I take a notion to pee on a pine tree in the back yard, which I do regularly. Perry, my bride of many years, tells me that I'm killing the trees doing that, but I think that's nonsense. She does point out, however, that my three favorite peeing trees have died over the years, and I've had to cut them down. I think it's pure coincidence, and I've carefully selected three more, and I'm keeping records. Besides, I don't know why anybody would want to live out in the country where nobody was close around if they couldn't pee on a tree once in a while. It's just a natural thing.

We used to raise a few soybeans on part of the place. The yield wasn't much to write home about until a strange thing happened one year long enough ago that I was scared to talk about until the statute of limitations had run out. Which it just did. A couple of Saturdays ago, I told the bunch down at the barber shop in Canton, which is the barber shop closest to Shocco, about the happening. By now, it's probably all over Canton, so I guess it can't hurt much more to tell you.

It all started when I built a barbed wire fence across a section line a little over seven years ago. See, my place lies in a couple of sections. (I'm talking about the SECTION, TOWNSHIP & RANGE kind of sections, like on a map. The place is all in one piece.) The section line running through the place used to be straight.

2

My papa told me one time when I was a tad helping him
stretch a fence, that you didn't want to stretch barbed wire (we
called it bob wire; I still do) too tight in the summer. Because if
you stretch it too tight, when winter comes and it gets cold, the
wire shrinks up and might break. But I was building this fence in
the winter and it was cold enough to freeze the balls off a pool
table. So I figured that if I didn't stretch it real tight when it was
cold, then the opposite reaction would happen in the summer
when the wire heated up, and the wire would get slack. And I like
my fences tight. Besides, I had just bought a new come-along,
and I wanted to really try it out. If you don't know what a come-
along is, it's a thing with a big wire cable and a ratcheting handle
that you hook to something solid and hook the wire onto the
cable and ratchet up 'til the wire gets tight. That's the best I can
do. If you still can't picture how it works, I'd just have to show
you one. Anyway, you can sure stretch bob wire tight with a big
one. And mine was big.

I had got a couple of great big utility poles that the utility
company had replaced and I'd cut them into eleven foot lengths
for my corner posts. I sunk them five feet in the ground and
anchored them in concrete. Perry also tells me that anything I
build is an overkill, but I don't like to build anything but once.
And I like my fences strong. Also, when you stretch wire tight
from one corner post to the other, the wire lies in a straight line
which you use as a guide to dig the fencepost holes to put the

regular fenceposts in to staple the wire to. It makes the fence straight. And I like my fences straight.

Well, I had hooked the come-along to one of the corner posts and had stretched the bottom two strands of wire and stapled them to the regular fence posts between the corner posts. The come-along was doing just like I hoped it would, because those strands were tight! And that fence was straight. If I'd wanted to, I could have laid a rifle on top of one corner post and shot at the top of the other corner post and the bullet would have notched the top of every regular post in the fence. I was getting ready to stretch the third strand when my helper happened to strum up on the two bottom wires with a stick. The sound was familiar. Sounded like the "MY DOG" part of "MY DOG HAS FLEAS." It was going to be a four strand fence, so I got to wondering if I could tune the top strands to play "HAS FLEAS." When I tightened the third "HAS" strand up to where it sounded right, I thought I heard a deep, rumbling groaning sound. I figured my helper had just eaten too much breakfast, and set about getting ready to stretch the "FLEAS" wire.

Now, the "FLEAS" note is higher than all three of the others, so this strand of bob wire had to be even tighter than the others. I had almost got it right on my initial stretching. I was just about a half note away. The wire was fairly quivering, and I didn't have the muscle to tighten one more click on the come-along ratchet. So I slipped a piece of pipe over the handle, making it longer to get more leverage, and hit it two more clicks. The wire sounded like it

4

was supposed to. I strummed up with the stick, and it sang "MY
DOG HAS FLEAS" as true as you please. That's when it
happened. The fence was so tight, it curved the section line. It's
been driving the county surveyors crazy ever since then trying to
figure out why that damn section line wasn't straight. And I've
lived in fear that I would get in some kind of trouble if the county
found out that I was responsible. But that was a little over seven
years ago, and I ain't worried about it now. The seven-year
statute of limitations has run out. The reason I know about this
statute of limitation is I overheard one of the smartest men in
Canton telling somebody about it, and he said that the seven-year
statute of limitations was based on the ancient Jewish law of
forgiving any debt that was seven years old. I dang sure don't
know any modern day Jews who do that now. Gentiles, either. I
wish to hell they did. Especially the Gentiles. 'Most all the money
I owe is to Gentiles. Seems to me that we throw away all the old
laws that make sense and pile on a bunch of new ones that don't.
But that's just my opinion, and not based on any study.

When the section line bent, the whole quarter mile of
ground between the corner posts wrinkled up in rows, kind of like
the forehead of a preacher who's just heard you say a cuss word.
You know how they do. They put their chin down on their chest
and raise their eyebrows and look at you out of the top of their
eyes, which wrinkles up their brow in a sort of condemning,
questioning look that says, "I really didn't hear what I thought I
heard, did I?" That's how that ground looked for about a ten-acre

5

strip on each side of the fence. Funny looking rows, but rows, nevertheless. Which got me to thinking. Since it was already rowed up, I could just plant the soybeans in the top of the rows and save a little money, not having to row the field up.

Well, the only thing I can figure happened is when the ground got squeezed like it did and pushed those rows up, the minerals and stuff got all mashed together pretty close and put more nutrients and the like within easy reach of each plant's roots. That crop of soybeans beat anything I'd ever seen up to then. Those soybeans grew to be big as hen eggs, and four to a pod. When I say big as hen eggs, I'm talking about the *average* size of those soybeans. My young'uns picked up one that they played regulation softball with for a full season. It was hard as a rock and was none the worse for wear when softball season was over. One of the kids evidently forgot to bring it in the house after the last game and it lay where it was thrown in a sunny spot on the east side of the house. We got a good soaking rain shortly thereafter, and the softball bean sprouted. I didn't know all this until one day I noticed more than usual shade on the east side. I walked around and was more than surprised at the size of the sprout. There was no question that the thing had to be cut down, or all the shade was going to kill the grass in about a quarter acre. My chain saw had just been sharpened, so I used it to cut the sprout down. Took me about an hour, and I had to get the chain saw resharpened after I finally got the plant cut down. I also managed to salvage three of the leaves. I took some measurements, and using tin snips, made three tarpaulins out of those leaves, each just the right size to cover the bed of my pickup truck. They lasted for years.

Now, I was amazed at that crop of beans, but it wasn't *anything* compared to the next year's crop. See, I saved most of those beans for seed. We planted them on those funny looking rows using a post hole digger to punch the holes to plant them in. That next year's crop was *something*. The beans were as big as volleyballs. We couldn't use a regular combine to cut those beans down. We had to take two bulldozers, stretch a big chain between them, move one dozer up a few yards and stop, and move the other dozer up even with the first so that the chain was cutting the plants down. Then the labor intensive part started. We had to take machetes, cut the pods open, and throw those volleyball sized beans up on the truck one at a time. In case you're interested, you can get a hernia throwing beans that big all day long.

Well, the whole thing turned into one big money-losing mess. After harvesting those beans, which as you can see was as tough a job as you'll ever want to get involved in, I had a field full of stumps that had to be cleared all over again just like it did when it was full of trees in the beginning. The labor costs of chunking those beans up on the trucks was out of sight, along with the doctor bills for all those hernias. And nobody would buy the beans because they didn't believe they were real soybeans.

I finally said to hell with it and piled all of those beans up and burned them. Then I cleared up all those stumps and replowed the field up and turned it into pasture. The county engineers evidently cheated and resurveyed the section line straight so they wouldn't have to explain why their prior figures never seemed to be accurate, and none of the county records even show that it was ever bent. That bunch is pretty close-mouthed, and none of them will even admit that they ever had a problem with that crazy line. And since I've burned the beans, there ain't a trace of their having ever existed. And, of course, the field is flat now, so the rows are gone. The short of it is that I can't actually prove that what I've told you is the truth. But the more I think about it, you haven't even asked me to prove anything, have you?

Perry gets on my case once in a while when I talk about those beans. She says that they weren't nearly as big as volleyballs and fusses about my growing beans like I grow bass and bird dogs. Only the biggest and the best. I guess she may have a point, and I'll reluctantly concede that they may not have been as big as volleyballs.

More like cantaloupes.

CHURCH MATTERS

If God has a sense of humor (and He must have, since He created us the way we are), He must kind of grin and shake His head when He watches us. Sort of like watching your five-year-old insisting that she choose her clothes and dress herself for the first time on the day she starts to feel kind of salty and experienced about getting ready for another day at kindergarten. Then she shows up with different colored socks, shoes on the wrong feet, a frilly pinafore over a pair of raggedy blue jeans, and she just loves the way she looks. I bet He views us like that. Especially when it comes to church matters. I'll give you an example, and you put yourself in His place and think about it.

I was born and reared a Southern Baptist. The first preacher I remember was a dapper, short, dynamic, get-things-done type of fellow named Brother Miller. He wore dark blue pinstripe Brooks Brothers-looking suits, always freshly pressed; an unblemished gray Homburg hat; spotless, heavily starched white dress shirts with cuff links; a natty tie; and drove the biggest Cadillac I'd ever seen. When he was around, folks felt a *presence*.

There had evidently been a pretty intensive search for a new pastor before he arrived, because there was a good bit of excitement in the Baptist community the first Sunday he was to preach in our church. I don't remember the sermon, but I do remember his standing up there in the pulpit and saying something like the church needed new carpet and new paint and new this, that, or the other, and that he would appreciate it if the congregation would search their hearts and come up with enough of a sacrifice to put the Lord's house in better shape. The appeal must have been fairly powerful, because one of the richest men in the church stood up and said, "I'll give a thousand dollars!" An audible gasp rippled through the church, because we're talking about the 1940s here, and a thousand dollars was a *passel* of money. Then another stood up and said, "I'll give five hundred," and so on. A lot of people were making pledges, and the numbers pledged were getting lower and lower as the not so fortunate made their intentions known. I had a dime, and I thought about pledging it until I remembered that I was almost out of BBs, and that dime had to last me for a week. I figured even the Lord wouldn't want my Red Ryder BB gun to be empty for a whole week.

Even without my dime, the church got spiffed up and the smell of new paint and the look and feel of new carpet and new, shiny floor tiles and clean walls and new pew cushions made everybody feel better about the church and about us all. Folks

entered with a new sense of pride (which I always thought
wenteth before a fall) and carefully moved about so as not to scar
a wall or muss up a pew cushion. New hymnbooks started taking
over the old raggedy ones and the pages had to be looked up now
rather than be turned to where the dog-eared ones had been
marked. The choir showed up one Sunday morning in blue robes
with those big circle-looking white collars, and sang two special
hymns instead of one, and the rest of us were impressed. I
wondered if they sounded better to God when they were all
dressed up in those robes rather than in just their Sunday
clothes, but I figured that Brother Miller had a more direct
pipeline than I did, and if he was behind all of this, it must be
right. I sure as Ned didn't want to be the one to pose a dumb
question like that to *him*.

He did everything right. The women loved him, the men
sought his counsel, and the children just absolutely quivered
when they were proffered a smile or a touch. I mean there was
some kind of fierce competition between the children to see who
could memorize more Bible verses in Sunday School or win at the
sword drill (looking up the books in the Bible in a hurry), or name
the books in order by heart. Ribbons were awarded by Brother
Miller in the church services to those who were lucky enough to
excel at those pursuits. Girls won almost all of the time. They
minced up the pulpit steps to receive the ribbons, modestly looked
down, but secretly glanced sideways from under those lowered
eyelids and smiled shadowy smiles which said, "I'm glad I'm not

dumb like you, Jimmy Ritchie." Long hair, big bows of ribbons, frilly dumb dresses, broomstick legs with bruises on the shins, and folded down lacy socks wrinkling into white patent leather shoes covering their big feet.

Once in a while a sissy won or somebody burdened with an oversized brain did. I didn't fit either of those categories, and to my best recollection, I never won one of those dumb ribbons. (Truth be known, I would secretly have killed for one, but would also have died of mortification if I'd won one.) My favorite verse was "Jesus wept," since it was easy to remember, being the shortest one in the Bible, and it was about the only one I ever used when called upon to recite. It started to wear pretty thin with the Sunday School teacher, but we didn't get report cards, and nobody I ever knew ever failed Sunday School, making the leverage the teacher had pretty weak. So the teacher endured the *Jesus wept*s, and as long as infractions in the class were kept as minor as untying the big sashes on dumb frilly dresses and making awful stretching faces and giggling, I and my hooligan friends in the class were allowed to simply attend while the teacher undoubtedly viewed us as her earthly crosses to bear and hoped for a more civilized bunch next year.

There was a short break of fifteen minutes or so between Sunday School and church services, so the boys scattered at the bell and headed for the churchyard to chase and holler. The upshot of this activity was a great many grass stains on the behinds and knees of Sunday britches as championship football

14

games, using a big paper cup for a football, or King of the Mountain (the Mountain being a slight mound where a stump had been removed) were played with all the fervor of a bunch of Samsons killing folks with the jawbone of an ass. (I remembered hearing that story, but somehow we all knew that we had better not use that word or the teacher would probably draw the line and tell parents and the live-and-let-live atmosphere would be shattered.)

Brother Miller didn't take much notice of me, since I never won any ribbons, nor did I ever really create enough of a problem in his presence to get him truly interested in my case.

Until my baptism.

Now, even those of you who are not Baptists probably know that when a Baptist is baptized, total and complete submersion is performed. I'm talking about all the way under so that you have to hold your breath, and don't wear a wig. (Friend of mine who is a Baptist preacher has a tale about a lady member who didn't get the word about wigs and had to retrieve hers in an unceremonious grabbing and splashing contest with the preacher to see who could lay hands on it first after it floated free when she was raised with Christ. But that's another story.)

Baptism is done in the name of the Father, the Son, and the Holy Ghost. For some reason, I have always figured that something that important, done in recognition of those names, ought to be done in *three* dips. In the name of the Father (dip), the Son (dip), and the Holy Ghost (dip). I bet it *was* done like that in the beginning. I reckon one reason why I feel so strongly about that is, I definitely went under three times when I was baptized. Two of them were unofficial, but I'll get to that in a minute. The other reason why if it was up to me I'd dip three times, is with all the sins hopefully being washed away from some folks I've seen being baptized, I ain't sure that one little dip could really do it. Three might. But then again, practically speaking, if *all* of them were washed away, it might possibly stain the water. And that might dampen the enthusiasm of the people waiting to be baptized next. More I think about it, judgement would have to be passed on who would dirty up the water more and put them at the back of the line, and judgement is frowned upon lest ye be judged. So I guess its all been thought out pretty clearly or perfected by trial and error throughout the ages. Besides, it ain't up to me and I don't know how I got off on theology anyway. So let's get back to the painful memories surrounding my baptism.

It all started one Sunday morning when I was about nine years old. One of my hooligan friends (name of Ralph) and I were sitting in the balcony of the church during preaching services. Most of the young'uns preferred to sit in the balcony so they wouldn't be under the constant scrutiny of parents and could fidget at least a little bit. Ralph and I were fidgeting a little more than generally acceptable and some pretty loud snickering and more than usual elbow-in-the-side-punching activity was going on. He and I had already received a couple of dark looks from each of our mothers down below in the congregation, and there

16

was no doubt in either of our minds that we were in for it after the service was over. Our only consolation at the time was that neither of our fathers had looked up there yet. We both knew that if we got a look from either of them, Christian attitudes took on a whole new meaning.

Well, Brother Miller was expounding on what must have been an important point about everybody scurrying around doing worldly things without stopping once in a while to listen to what God was trying to tell us all, because he fairly hollered, "**HUSH, AND BE STILL,**" and was looking up right at me and Ralph. Me and Ralph hushed and got still. And noticed that both of our fathers were looking up at us. And frowning.

That's when I got saved.

Ralph, too.

When the end of the sermon was reached and the invitation was issued to surrender all and join the church and the invitational hymn was being sung, I got up and made my way down to the front of the church to make my intentions known. I didn't know Ralph was right behind me until I was halfway down the balcony steps. I looked around and saw his pale face and eyes that said to me without his having to verbalize, "You ain't leaving me up there alone. Besides, it's a better idea than anything I got."

We marched right up to Brother Miller, who smiled and shook our hands, and had us stand by him after the hymn so that the congregation could come by and greet us as new converts and members. Everybody was smiling and gracious and we got hugs and handshakes and special, misty-eyed hugs from our parents.

Now before you get all righteous and start mouthing things like "hypocritical" and "opportunistic" and other unlovely adjectives, you need to remember that He works in strange and mysterious ways. I'm sure that's what my mother was thinking and probably hoping. Anyway, a very positive atmosphere displaced a potentially very negative one and it worked out pretty well. My hooligan attitude was displaced by one of a more serene nature for a couple of days and my behind was immeasurably better off.

Baptism services in our church were performed once each month at a Sunday night service. The baptistry was an aquarium-like apparatus located behind the pulpit up above the choir loft. The front of the baptistry was a pane of glass which allowed you to see a foot or so of the water where the baptizing was taking place. Steps usually led down into the baptistry on one end and up out of it at the other end. It was about four and a half feet deep. Our baptistry was getting its share of the renovation work going on at the church, and the steps had been temporarily removed. A semi-gradual slope consisting of a corrugated metal walkway had been installed at each end to substitute for steps until they could be put in. And the walkways were a little slippery.

The lights in the church were dimmed except for the ones in the baptistry, which lent additional drama to the event.

In the late afternoon of my baptismal Sunday, Mama summoned me in from the woods to get ready. She explained that I would change out of my clothes at the church and don a white robe for the baptism. After the service, I would dry off with the towel she provided for me, and change back into my brand new Sunday clothes. Since this was winter time, the Sunday britches were made out of a hard, heavy, scratchy wool material. I distinctly remember that.

We got to the church a little early like we were instructed to do. I took the towel, separated from my family, and headed for the room where we were supposed to change into our white robes. Ralph was already there. And he was worried. "You can't see through these robes when they're dry," he said, "but when they get wet, I ain't too sure about how much they cover up."

"Ralph, nobody can see from your chest down anyway when you get in the water, and nobody but you and me can see you when you get out," I said.

"Brother Miller can."

I hadn't thought about that. Or the possibility that somebody might be assigned to assist us when we returned from the holy event.

"Well, I'm fixing to wear my drawers under that robe," I said.

"They'll get wet," he cautioned. I was getting a little frayed with him. "Who cares? How many times at the swimming hole have your drawers got wet or muddy and you just wore your britches home with no drawers underneath? A bunch of times, I bet, and this won't be any different. Nobody but you and me will know we don't have no drawers on."

"God will know."

"He won't care."

So we left our drawers on under the robes and proceeded to the walkway leading down into the baptistry to await our cue to be baptized.

Brother Miller was already in the baptistry, giving a short message to the congregation. I was to go first, so I had a good look at him from my vantage point slightly above him. And a mystery cleared up for me. I had never understood how he managed to get out of that baptistry after a service and get back to the pulpit in such a hurry without being the slightest bit damp and with his Brooks Brothers suit and starched white shirt still impeccable. Now I did! He was wearing chest waders like you duck hunt in under his robe! And I also noticed that since he was pretty short, the water was only about a couple of inches below the top of the waders and that he was standing sort of tippy-toed to keep it at that level, making his balance not too steady.

The plan was, when Brother Miller finished his remarks and was ready for me to come down, he was to look up at us, nod, and outstretch one arm toward us. I was not paying too much attention to what he was saying, since I was surveying the congregation through a little crack between the wall and a small curtain behind which I stood, trying to pick out my parents in the darkened area. Brother Miller looked up at us, nodded, and stretched out his beckoning arm. I was still looking through the crack. Things got quiet. Ralph said, "Jimmy, G'WONE!" (Rhymes with "bone"—little boy Southern for "go on"). I said, "What?"

"G'WONE!!!!"

I snapped a look at Brother Miller and realized that the whole world was waiting for my next move. I reckon that pressure was the reason my first step was too long. My heel slipped on that walkway and I went slap under. I managed to grab something structural and stand up, but when I did, I was halfway between the usual starting point where the congregation could first glimpse the entering, and Brother Miller. So the first sight they had of me was not the usual dignified entering, but rather my rising from the water like a drowned rat. With a little splashing and coughing.

Brother Miller didn't look too happy, but there was no turning back now. He washed my sins away with a practiced, smooth dip, and turned me loose. I waded the couple of steps to the other incline and started out. But I reckon the Lord figured I wasn't quite sinless yet, 'cause I almost got to the top of the incline and slipped down again. This time I reached above my head in a futile attempt to grab onto anything. The motion caused me to straighten my whole body and turn into a wet, sinless, nine-year-old, underwater projectile. I shot back down that incline following the contour of the bottom, robe flaring over my head, with straight legs locked at the knees.

Both feet caught Brother Miller on the side of his left leg somewhere about knee level. Just right. Unfortunately. He disappeared from the congregation's sight as his legs were knocked sideways like a bowling pin and under he went.

Things got confusing for me. I was under water with that damn robe over my head, and there was a lot of thrashing around me that I didn't cause. On purpose. Brother Miller was having the same problem, I reckon, but I ain't sure his robe was creating problems for him like mine was for me. I'm sure his waders were full, though. After he disappeared, the congregation couldn't see anything but the baptistry water sloshing up against the glass pane and maybe occasionally a hand or a foot or a boot. Ralph was the only one who saw the whole thing. He made a mental note to watch out on the slippery inclines when his turn came.

I finally figured out which way was up and got the hell out of there, half crawling up the incline and choking and coughing and not looking back. I had finished drying off and was half dressed when Ralph came in, dripping, newly sinless, and grinning.

"Did you get baptized?", I asked, nonchalantly.

"Yep. But not as much as you did. He held me under a lot longer than I thought he needed to, though. And he dang sure didn't look too happy."

Well, I'm going to shorten the rest of this, now. I don't need to tell you how hard, scratchy wool britches feel without drawers, how I made sure that Ralph was between me and Brother Miller when we lined up in the church to accept the congratulatory handshakes and hugs from the congregation, or how I wondered if Brother Miller had brought an extra pair of drawers, since he still looked pretty damp. I've thought about this event a lot in the ensuing years, sometimes with embarrassment and sometimes with hesitantly humorous feelings. But what I think ain't too important, I guess. I just wonder what God thought. Or thinks.

BARBER SH

Razor Cuts & Hair Styling

OPEN

DISJOINTED RAMBLINGS ABOUT AN INSTITUTION REVISITED

You know what I miss? The old-time barber shop. I miss the rows and rows of different colored hair tonic bottles, the striped revolving barber pole, the unhurried atmosphere of the male center of the community where all the news was disseminated by the barber who knew everything about everybody (or at least appeared to), the shine stand with the steel soles atop long metal rods where you placed your feet if your legs were long enough, the smells of leather, shoe polish, hair tonic, talcum powder, soaps, and warm lather whipped up in a mug by a practiced hand with a shaving brush.

I miss the measured slap, slap, slap of a straight razor being honed to a perfect edge on a big old razor strop, and just the general feeling of comradery which always seemed to prevail in that setting.

The banter was unceasing, and woe to the individual in one of the chairs who had a thin skin about his bird dog which had run up three straight coveys, or who was known to have a fair case of hem'roids, or who had lost a bet on the high school football game, or whose son had just beat him for the first time in a game of straight pool. The good-natured kidding sometimes bordered on getting a little rough, but it never seemed to be vicious when it was done in the barber shop. That kind of talk was just expected.

There was a lot of positive chatter, too. I can remember walking into the barber shop with my Daddy, the top of my head not quite reaching his beltline, and hearing the barber, Commodore Smith, (real name) loudly greeting us with "Come on in, Red. I see you brought your bodyguard with you. Have a seat over there, young man, and I'll get to you in just a few minutes. I've got a haircut just your size, and I've been saving it all day just for you." I'd feel a foot taller than I had seconds before. I was all of a sudden a man in a man's place.

Women, in those days, were a little out of place in a barber shop. Sometimes one would sort of half apologetically come in with a toddler in tow to get his hair cut, and the conversation would mute somewhat. The language I remember pervading the barber shop was never foul even if a female was not present, but things quieted down noticeably while she was there. There seemed to be a general, unspoken sigh of relief when the little boy's haircut was completed and she left and things returned to normal. That may not set well with some of the feminists, and I ain't saying it was exactly right, but that's the way it was. (And still is in some places.)

I guess the reason why women sort of stopped things was that we never quite knew how they would react to some stuff. I still don't know how even the gal I married will react to some things, and I've been fortunate enough to live with her for twenty-six years at the time of this writing. (I hope to prolong that condition from now on.)

You may say that the kidding and banter would have the same effect on a woman as it has on a man. It might. But take the conversation I had in a little barber shop on the town square in Canton not too long ago. Charley was the barber. Charley also talks a lot.

The top of my head is getting pretty slick. Somebody told me once that in places, he doesn't see how a fly could light on it without slipping off. On a particular Saturday morning, (Saturday mornings are generally the busiest time for barber shops in small towns), my turn finally came to climb into the chair for what can only be called a cruelty joke. The shop was packed. I told Charley that I had been giving a matter some serious thought, and he and the crowd got pretty interested in any matter to which I would give any thought at all, let alone any serious thought. Things quieted down pretty quick. "What is it?" Charley wanted to know.

"Charley, I think I ought to get a discount."

Charley backed off, rubbed his hand over his chin, and appeared to be digging down pretty deep.

Finally he said, "Jim, I guess I can understand how you might feel that way. But if you look at it from my side, I really think I should charge you more than the going rate. You've heard all your life that scrappin' is harder than pickin'. Besides, I don't even like to cut your hair. I've seen better hair than yours on salt meat."

Well, the barber shop exploded in knee-slapping laughter. I acted sorry I had brought the subject up, and grinned and admitted that he was probably right. But can you imagine what would have happened if he had told that to a woman? Think about it. You ain't sure, and Charley wouldn't have been sure either, so he wouldn't have said it. He'd have stumbled and fumbled around and said something like, "Yes ma'am, I probably ought to give you a discount because I really like to cut your hair, but I just can't." See?

The one thing that has improved is that the barbers these days don't use the loud smelling hair tonic they once did as a matter of course. When I was a boy, before you knew it, the barber would slosh about four of five squirts of sweet smellum on your head that would draw every fly in the county as you walked home. That meant that you always washed your head the night of the day you got a haircut. Mama would not let me put my head on no pillowcase of hers smelling like that.

A barber shop is the one place where, in a matter of minutes, a baby becomes a boy. I remember distinctly the first time my firstborn got his first haircut. The blond curls and ringlets surrounded his head in a fine, wispy halo that had "baby" written all over it. He was a fine, chubby, dimpled little baby. After the haircut, he was a stocky, husky, look-'em-straight-in-the-eye little *boy* who looked ready to rip and roar. He had toddled into the shop. Under that new haircut, that same gait took on the appearance of a swagger. I was as proud of him then as the day I found out that I was a father. Or the day years later when he called me from medical school to tell me that he had delivered his first baby.

His mother wasn't too keen on the new haircut when I brought him home, but he and I rassled on the floor more than usual that night. The baby had left.

I vividly remember lots of experiences that happened in an old-time barber shop. Like the Saturday night I accompanied my daddy on another trip to Mr. Smith's shop so he could get a shave after a particularly hard day. Mr. Smith leaned the barber chair back into a prone position with my father in it, whipped up the lather in the mug, brushed it thickly on, wrapped Papa's face in a steamy towel so that only his nose was showing, and sat down with some of the other patrons to chat. The shop was full, but nobody seemed to be in a hurry. I remember that I began to fidget after a while, worrying that Mr. Smith had forgotten my daddy and let him smother to death under that big, steaming hot towel.

I wasn't sure that enough of his nose was sticking out to allow him to breathe. And he sure was still. It was a relief to see Mr. Smith, after about five minutes, go over to Papa and replace the towel with another one. I heard Papa mumble something, so I knew he wasn't dead after all. Mr. Smith chatted for another five minutes or so, then unwrapped the towel, lathered Papa up for a second time, honed the razor with about a dozen slaps on the strop, and began the careful, deliberate, skillful process of shaving. When he finished, after much stroking of the face to ensure that there were no rough spots, he massaged Papa's neck and shoulder muscles, slapped some Old Spice on him and whipped the cloth off. Papa wasn't smiling, but I could tell that he wanted to. He smelled good, and his face was smooth as a spanked baby's behind. I know, because he picked me up and hugged me as we left, after having paid Mr. Smith his six bits.

My first personal encounter with a straight razor in a barber shop occurred in Houma, Louisiana. My little brother, Johnny, and I went to get a haircut in a little shop not too far from where we lived at the time, right after we moved to Houma. There were two barbers in the shop, and no other customers when we arrived, so we each climbed into a chair. The barbers worked at about the same speed, and when the one working on me lathered around my ears to define what was to be in the future, sideburns, I glanced over at Johnny to be sure he was watching. There he sat, chin down on his chest, slicing a sideways glance at me, also lathered around the ears, and with lips pulled back under his teeth to suppress a grin. We had been sort of shaved! With a straight razor! In a barber shop! And we giggled all the way home.

Now, I've told a pretty big lie here. I really don't miss the old-time barber shop so much any more. Charley's Barbershop on the square closed some time ago, but there's another shop on the square in Canton. It used to be the old hotel's barber shop. Bobby Chandler and Danny Joe O'Cain run the place and there ain't a pastel color in it. There's a stuffed deer head and a stuffed bobcat in it. The old shoeshine stand sits where it has for years. The shoeshine expert who works there still applies polish with his fingers, and can make the shine rag pop with a flourish. Today's newspaper is scattered in sections throughout the row of waiting chairs and a stack of dogeared *Outdoor Life* and *Sports Afield* and *Field and Stream* and *Sports Illustrated* magazines beckon. A big rattlesnake skin is stretched down one corner. There is a sign on the wall that says, "Cows may come, and cows may go, but the bull in here goes on forever." Folks chatter and laugh and the humor is rough on thin skins. Hot dang! I love that place!

GRANDPARENTS

Whoever named them knew what he (or she) was doing. They could have just as easily been called wonderful-parents or wiseparents or superduperparents. Roll the experiences of raising one set of young'uns into the wisdom of living long enough to separate the really important facets of life from the superficial things, and you generally come up with a pattern for grandparents' way of dealing with their grandchildren. And that brings up another subject. You will notice that grandparents' children are called the *children*. The children's children are called *grand*children. Now this name, no doubt, was initiated by a grandparent who, as most grandparents do, view their second generation offspring as superduperchildren. Sort of a mutual admiration society with the first generation children simply acting as middlemen to get the other two together. You can even carry this thought further when you add yet another generation called great-grandparents. That name fits too. So does great-great, and so on.

Grandparents just *know* more about children, life, the Great Depression, World War II, the Bible, skinned knees, where the fish might be biting, the sunniest bench in the park, dogs and cats, old-timey Tarzan movies, and Grimm's Fairy Tales. You know...the *important* things.

My grandparents knew lots of good stuff. At least the three with whom I was privileged to spend a part of my younger life did. I never knew my paternal grandfather, who expired of a gunshot wound some seventeen years before I was born. Some folks say that this unhappy event occurred as a result of a fiery temper and impulsive nature and that it was deserved, but I won't get into that here. Some folks also say that I "take after" him, which makes me a little nervous around the ones who say that he got his just desserts.

The others passed to their rewards prior to my reaching my teens, but in those short years, a bond was developed which to this day remains strong and very dear. I sometimes still talk to them and often believe I get answered. Not the hands-on-the-table-listening-for-the-chandelier-to-rattle kind of talk, but just a quiet, non-verbal chat, swapping a few mental grins.

They were typical grandparents, I guess, spoiling us rotten and allowing us to do things which would have been unthinkable for my parents to have done. Overprotective, seeing no wrong, bragging on our least accomplishments, and pouring out love in oversized doses, they were a haven for the whole bunch of us brothers and sisters and cousins. There was always a lap to crawl

up into and a willing ear to listen to any lament or new discovery or outlandish, childish statement of absolute fact. Example: "Mawmaw, did you know that a coachwhip snake will run faster than I can, and if he catches me, could whip me to death with his tail, and tie me up with the little part of his tail, and break it off and grow another one, and look for somebody else to do it to?"

"No, I didn't know that. How did you know that?"

"I just *know*."

"Well, then, I expect that you'd better stay away from those coachwhip snakes, don't you?"

No chastisement like "Now, Jimmy, that's not so." They would most of the time let you get away with a big one like that unless it was truly harmful, and, since you received no rebuttal, you might get to thinking that at least part of it might be true. Which could cause some wonderment. Which ain't all bad.

When we were at my grandparents' houses, everybody generally played by their rules, including my parents. I can remember using my paternal grandmother's bed for a trampoline when I was about five, and having an uncle tell me to stop. Mama Ritchie (who knows why we named them the things we did?) flew all over him. "You let that baby alone!"

"Now Mama," my uncle said, "you wouldn't have let any of us do that when we were his age."

"I probably wouldn't have," she admitted, "but you have to be sixty years old before you know how to raise children. It's a shame that raising children has to be done by young folks who don't have sense enough to do it right." My uncle backed off. And those creaking bedsprings continued to send me higher than anyone had ever been before.

While Mama Ritchie was a firecracker with a pretty short fuse with everybody but grandchildren, Mawmaw was just as hickory tough, but much more softspoken. I never saw her really bristle but once, and I'll get to that later. I still wonder how that beautiful, gentle person got linked up with my Pawpaw. I guess opposites attract, to coin a phrase.

Pawpaw was my hero of the known world. He was a tall, thin, dark whip of a man who was a carpenter by trade. His corded forearms, which were always exposed because he always rolled the cuffs of his shirts up twice, even dress shirts, were encased in the smoothest, most translucent skin I have ever seen on a man. The things he could do with a hammer and handsaw were marvelous. Ends were cut square and joints fit tight. His hammer could and often did swing all day long with those blue veined hands and arms never seeming to tire or grow careless. He rolled his own cigarettes using OCB papers and Prince Albert tobacco, and he always let me have his empty Prince Albert cans. I could cuss a little in his presence if the womenfolk or my daddy weren't around, and on Sundays after church, my brother and I would crawl up into his lap and he'd read the funnies to us. The secondmost thing I remember about him was that he always seemed to have time for me, whether it was to get him a dipper of water when it would probably have been easier for him to get it

himself, or to fetch him some nails two or three times until I got the right size, or any number of little tasks which made me a seemingly important part of his efforts. The firstmost thing I remember about him was something he told me, and I'll get to that in a minute.

I'll duck away from my people briefly and introduce you to my wife's maternal grandparents, two of the neatest people I've ever known.

They were curious people. I don't mean strange curious, I mean inquisitive curious. Nello was a school teacher and Moseley, a large, robust man with a thatch of white hair and a white mustache, was the editor of a large company newspaper. And both were wonderful, witty, wise people with an insatiable desire to learn new things. Both full of stories and poetry and humor. It was normal to see them both sitting in the middle of the floor surrounded by many open volumes of the encyclopedia scattered because one of them would look something up in one volume, see something there that would pique their interest in another or related subject which needed looking up in another volume, and these required chaining to another, and so on. And they would be *excited* about it.

Moseley once got to wondering about the finer points of catching shrimp, so he spent a month on a shrimp boat, just to learn. I had the opportunity once to slip off with him to a farm pond to do a little fishing. He tired pretty quickly in the little boat (especially since the fish weren't cooperating) and he

39

suggested that I continue on, but let him out on the bank so he could stretch a bit and see what damage he could do to the fish population with his cane pole. I did so, and after a few minutes, glanced over to where I'd let him out. He was not in sight, and the fishing pole was unattended. I paddled toward the pole and caught a glimpse of that white hair just above the calf-high grass. He had had a touch of heart trouble in the recent past, and this whirled through my mind as I paddled furiously over toward him. As I got closer, I could see that he was lying on his side facing away from me with his elbow on the ground and his head cradled in his propped-up hand. I beached the boat, and casually walked up behind him, scared to death that he was having a problem. He was intently studying an ant hill and the antics of the occupants. He didn't even know that I was around until my shadow fell across the ant hill. Then he began explaining to me what he had observed about the patterns of travel of the ants. I mean he was interested in *everything*. Especially young people, with whom he loved to play a tough, competitive game of chess or just talk. And he had the art of listening to us. Nello and Moseley were a joy to be around.

I told you earlier that I'd get around to the memorable statement I got from Pawpaw and the only time I saw Mawmaw really bristle. Both happened in the space of ten minutes. Pawpaw was, as I mentioned, a carpenter by trade, but he was also a county deputy sheriff. And he did truly love deputy sheriffing. He also loved reading those old detective story pulp magazines while sitting in his squeaky rocking chair out on the front porch. My little brother and I used to crawl up in his lap and pester him into reading aloud the story he happened to be reading at the time. He never cut the gory details out of those stories, but just read them out as they were written. Which was not to the liking of Mawmaw. She'd be in the house doing something which would cause her to pass by the front door. From there she could hear what he was reading, and if it was too rough, she'd gently admonish him about reading such stuff to "those babies." He'd agree and roll up the magazine and shove it between the rocking chair braces under him, and begin rocking and talking about other things. Until Mawmaw was out of earshot. Then we'd pick up where we were when we were interrupted. Except one time.

This story, which I don't remember, must have been pretty rough. She had gone through her admonishment, he had rolled up the magazine and stuck it under the rocker, then brought it out again, had been caught again, and the admonishment became a little more severe. For the second time the magazine was rolled up and then unrolled. The third time, she put on a show. I was flabbergasted. I didn't know he would allow anybody, including Mawmaw, to talk to him that way, but that time he did. I noticed a kind of twinkle in his eye as he listened, like he kind of enjoyed seeing her riled a bit so she could let some steam out. Then he agreed with her and closed the magazine in a way that let us know this story session was over. When she bustled back into the house, he looked at me and must have read my thoughts, which were "Why in the world...?"

He said, "Boy, if you ever get old enough to get married, and it's questionable at this point whether you'll live that long," (I was pretty bad, even at that age, about getting into trouble myself) "you'll find that there are two kinds of husbands. Them that's henpecked... and them that lie about it." The older I get, the smarter my Pawpaw was.

It's been many years since the last one of them departed this life. I still miss them. I delight in the certain feeling that on one great day, I'll see them again.

SOMETIMES THINKING BACK
AIN'T ALL THAT GOOD

M ost folks love to think back on earlier times. You know... when times were good and problems were few and joints didn't ache and you could identify cars by sight without having to read the logo on them. When you could actually talk to somebody in a normal tone of voice at the same time music was being played and they could hear you. When those who had their own car at college were the exception and only the rich kids or the ones who worked after school at gas stations had one in high school. When you first discovered that girls smelled good up close. When barbershops proudly displayed a sign on the plate glass window certifying that the place was air conditioned. Remember those signs? They had a sort of icebergy motif and the sign said "**IT'S COOL INSIDE!!!**" with the icebergy stuff dripping all over the word **COOL**.

Well, I like to think back about the good times too. But for some unexplained reason, when I get to thinking about the good times, some of the other times begin to creep in, and pretty soon, they just get clearer and clearer, until they take over center stage.

Take high school football, for instance. I was a junior when our Natchez High School won the South Mississippi Big 8 Championship. And I made lots of good tackles and good blocks. Unfortunately, most of our real athletes were seniors and graduated after that year, leaving a few great athletes and a whole bunch of us not-so-great (actually, not so good).

Our coach, however, had grandiose ideas of repeating the record, regardless of our talent, so he scheduled our opening game the next year with a large out-of-state town who had a super team. They had two high school All American running backs, for example, and we had several like me who could almost run the hundred in twenty seconds (without pads).

I played guard my senior year except when we punted (many times), or when we tried an extra point (very few times). On punts and extra points, I played center and snapped the ball because our first string center could not see a distance of over three feet without glasses or contact lenses, and in those days, you didn't wear either when you were playing football because only a sissy wore a face mask. And he was no sissy. In fact, he was pretty testy about the placement of the quarterback's hands when we ran plays from the "T" formation. Not that the quarterback was a sissy either.

Back to the ball game. The big town won the toss and elected to receive. Both of the All Americans were lined up deep to receive. One of them was tall, elusive, and the fastest kid any of us had ever seen. We will call him "Speedy." The other was plenty fast, but was shorter and strong and fearless. We will call him "Shorty."

Speedy took the opening kickoff on his five yard line and raced ninety-five yards without anyone even so much as touching him. They were ahead seven to nothing before ten seconds had run off the clock. Then they kicked off to us and we ran three downs and punted. And it went like that all night. They would score and we would take the kickoff and run three and punt.

Speedy and Shorty always lined up deep to receive. If Speedy received the punt, he and Shorty would cross, and Speedy always faked a hand off to Shorty. If Shorty received the punt, he and Speedy would cross, and he would hand the ball off to Speedy. Speedy always ran the punt back. Always. And he always ran the punt back a *long* way. He humiliated us. We were a very frustrated Defending South Big 8 Championship team. So when the score got lopsided enough to erase any hope of winning or even making a show of the thing, the name of the game became "**KILL SPEEDY**." We had to salvage something.

Now, they had apparently scouted us pretty well, because they knew how fast I was. This was evidenced by the fact that nobody was playing on my nose when I centered for a punt, and nobody bothered to block me as I went down the field to try and catch Speedy. It was pitiful. Sort of like an English bulldog trying to catch a greyhound. *Pitiful*, I'm telling you. I devised a plan. The one bright spot on our team was our punter. He could kick it high or he could kick it long, and sometimes he even did both. It was late in the game and when we had run our usual three downs and it was time to punt for the umpteenth time, I asked our punter to kick it high. And not too long. That way I figured I might be able to get down under it and have a semblance of a chance. He kicked a beauty. It was a real high, lazy punt that seemed to hang forever, which was about the time it took me to get within the neighborhood of the reception. Even then, they had time to get the ball and cross. I was close enough to aim for one step past the point of crossing where Speedy would be. It worked! I hit Speedy at a dead run just after they crossed, and never in the history of the sport had a lick like that been passed. I mean I heard all sorts of things pop and crack, and some of the things weren't mine. He didn't get up, and I didn't want to. But I figured as hard as he was hit, and as still as he was, the loose football had to be around somewhere, so I was scrambling around in a haze on my hands and knees looking for it. The crowd was going wild. Oh, the **GLORY** of it all!! I couldn't find the ball for some reason, and happened to look downfield from my hands and knees position. The discovery was awful.

What they were going wild about was that Shorty was streaking down the sidelines headed for yet another six points. The bastard had handed the ball off. And there I was, in front of God and everybody, with nobody within twenty yards of me and Speedy and Shorty at the place of action, and I had tackled the wrong man. That one play is the mainmost thing I remember about my football days. I still want to get sort of lost when I think about it. My coach did tell me when I managed to stagger off the field that I had made a good tackle. I guess he was sort of frustrated too.

How about the good old college days? Normally thinking about them conjures up thoughts about deep, philosophical conversations and parties and lifting tankards of ale in a rathskeller while lustfully singing fraternity songs a la the Student Prince.

Well, Ole Miss in those days didn't have a rathskeller. Hell, we had to go thirty miles to Holly Springs or thirty miles in the other direction to Marks just to buy a beer. Lafayette County was dry, you see.

We had just finished mid-semester finals in the spring semester of my freshman year, and we decided that the tests had caused enough wear and tear on us to justify a little diversion. A bunch of us good old tried and true frat brothers opted to head for Lambert's Grocery for said diversion. This place was a little clapboard semi-grocery just across the county line in Marks, Mississippi. I say semi-grocery because the front part of the building was set up with two or three booths next to a pockmarked picture window looking out onto an expanse of gravel. In the middle of this unlovely expanse, about twenty feet from the window, stood two bedraggled gas pumps guarding the building from the highway. The gravel area was lighted by two bright lights directly over the gas pumps. The part of the building not taken up with booths housed the groceries and a meat market. Talk about a class place to drink beer! You could get baloney and cheese and crackers and gas and beer and everything without ever having to leave the premises. And when we settled in there, we almost never left the premises until it was time to head back to school.

The booths were semi-circular devices which held about five or six people if you scrunched up pretty close. Which made it a pretty good place to take a date, because a trip to Lambert's always turned into a group affair, providing for a fair amount of scrunching. I didn't have a date on this particular trip, thank God, but I was in the middle of scrunching anyway.

The tight space in the booths did have one disadvantage. When you had to take a biological break and adjourn to the rest room, you had to squeeze out past the other scrunchers and lose your seat. So you held off the inevitable until the last possible second before your bladder parted at the seams and the baggy parts under your eyes were sweating in protest. Then you said something profound like "'Scuse me," and squeezed out, trying to be as nonchalant as possible as you headed for the door, knowing that you had a maximum of five or six seconds to get to the men's room before a catastrophe happened. That men's room had to be one of the most pleasant places in the world, even if you were forced to stand in a shallow puddle of what you hoped was water in front of the lidless, chipped toilet. The sheer relief was indescribable, and the prose you were able to read on the walls was passable. One of the inscriptions I remember was comprised of three parts. "I love grils," under which, in a different handwriting was "It's spelled g-i-r-l-s, stupid," under which, in a tiny scrawl was "Well, what about us grils?"

On this particular trip, we had arrived at Lambert's at about four p.m., and had imbibed until about eight, when the dating couples began to arrive and the serious scrunching began. I was sitting, as I recall, in the middle seat in one of the booths, and my last trip to the men's room had been history for a couple of hours. Nature had long since ceased to call. It was screaming. I reluctantly "'Scused" myself and began the familiar route to the men's room. By this time, the fact that the route was familiar was important, because my sense of direction along with all other senses except for the one which was causing this action had been all but destroyed by the quantity of beer which I had consumed in the last four hours. In short, my motor skills were severely impaired. The familiar route was to go out the front door, turn left to the corner of the building, turn left again, and the men's room was the first door on the left.

On this particular trip, however, something went wrong. It may have been that someone could have been coming in the front door as I was going out and they could have turned me around or something. In any event, I got lost outside and couldn't find the men's room. The bladder was threatening to explode and I for sure didn't have time to find the front door again to ask for help. So I did the only thing I could do at the time. I hid, unzipped, and let fly, thanking God that I was male and could act pretty casual about leaning on something with one hand with the other hand on my hip so that the cars passing behind me would have no idea that the act was being performed. Problem was, as my good old tried-and-true fraternity brothers gleefully told me later, that what I was leaning on was one of the gas pumps. I was hidden pretty securely between the pumps in the lighted area. And since I was concerned about having my back to the passing cars on the highway, I was pointing directly at the picture window.

Conversation in the booths, as I learned later, pretty well halted while some stared dumbfounded and others rolled their eyes at the ceiling and adjusted hairdos and cleared throats and planned the next hopefully benign topics of conversation. The biggest problem in the aftermath of the episode was that I couldn't remember who had been there when I put on my involuntary performance. So for weeks, when I met a coed walking on campus, I was sure I saw a knowing smirk on her face, and I didn't know whether to smile hello or turn red. I felt like I had no secrets from anyone. It was a hell of a feeling. Still is. I'm turning red now. So much for rathskellers and fraternity songs.

My Army days provided for lots of fond memories. Marriage, my firstborn son, officers' clubs and good, lifelong friends. Fond memories...except for...well, we'll call him Luzon to keep him anonymous.

Luzon was a special case. The people who created Gomer
Pyle had to have patterned him after Luzon because the
similarities are so incredibly striking.

I was a brand spanking new Second Lieutenant when I
arrived fresh from artillery school to the Second Infantry Division.
The Indian Head Division, as the Second was known because of
their shoulder patch, was at that time a boot training outfit. This
meant that we took raw recruits and made soldiers of them. Or
tried to, in Luzon's case.

It wasn't that he was a real problem. I mean, he didn't go
AWOL or get into fights or steal or malinger or anything like that.
He was one of the most pleasant people I've ever met.

Luzon was a long, tall drink of water from east Tennessee,
and he was in a group of trainees assigned to our battery for Boot
Camp. He thought that was wonderful. He was assigned to us
again for his Advanced Individual Training in artillery, and he
thought that was wonderful. He thought I was wonderful, that
the army was wonderful, that Fort Benning was wonderful. He
would had felt the same way about the Navy, the Marines, the
Foreign Legion, or Siberia, I reckon. I never saw him in a bad
mood.

But he was still a problem, and he was *my* problem, since he
was assigned to one of my sections. Military courtesy was beyond
him. He couldn't understand why he should salute you when it
was much more pleasant to holler at you from across the street,

run over, smile, shake your hand, and chat for a minute if you had time.

"Boy, Lieutenant Ritchie, you sure look nice. I never saw boots shine like that. How you do that? I mean you look sharp!" What do you do with somebody like that? I tried chewing him out.

"Private Luzon, the next time you fail to salute me and act like something other than a soldier around me, I'm going to run your butt around that parade field until you'll hate the very thought of ever seeing me again."

"Shoot, Lieutenant Ritchie, I couldn't feel like that about you. You're my friend. But I'll try to remember. I appreciate you trying to help me and teach me to do right. I surely do. Good to see you." Then he'd back off and smile and give the best salute he could and be very proud of the fact that he remembered that little nicety.

Our battery commander, a Captain, a gung-ho, stickler-for-detail type who had come up the hard way through Officer's Candidate School, was as much at a loss about what to do with Luzon as I was, but he at least had my fanny to chew out about him. And he chewed on my fanny regularly about Luzon.

One Friday afternoon we had the troops formed up when word came down that the Division Artillery Commander, a one-star General, was headed for the area and that he wanted to inspect one of the batteries. We were one of about a dozen batteries formed up, so our chance of having to go through with that bit of harassment was pretty small. (It probably wasn't harassment in the General's mind, but it sure was in ours.) All of us had to stay put until the General made up his mind which outfit he wanted to inspect.

Well, we were all standing around in place, chapped at the delay and grumbling a little, but relaxed because our chance of being the chosen outfit was so small. All but the Captain. The fact that the General was in the same hundred acres with us always caused his pucker factor to tighten measurably. He was scurrying around checking and rechecking and rechecking some more. And getting paler and paler. His worst fears were realized when the sedan with the flags on the front fenders pulled into our battery area and the General got out. It was to be our honor.

While the Captain ran up to report to the General, the First Sergeant got the troops lined up straight and we were ready by the time the dignitaries arrived. The Executive Officer's post and my post were at the rear of the battery, so we had a pretty good position from which to observe.

The First Sergeant preceded the General, who was followed by the Captain, as they started down the ranks. The General was asking the usual questions you would expect a General to ask privates. "What's your name, son?"; "What's your serial number?"; "How much money do you make?"; "What's your third General Order?"

Luzon was in the second rank, and I was watching his back. He was trying mightily not to perceptively turn his head to get a better view, but it was rough on him. The General finished with the first rank and turned down the second. He spoke to every fifth man, so the chance of his actually speaking to Luzon was not too great, and I thanked Providence for those odds. He was in full stride just prior to reaching Luzon, but for some devilish reason, he sort of paused, and then turned to face Luzon, eyeball to eyeball. I thought the Captain was going to have a serious stroke. The whole battery stiffened. Except Luzon. He was absolutely delighted, since he had never seen a General up that close.

"What's your name, son?"

"Private E-1 Luzon, sir!" semi-smiling in deference to all of the ribbons earned by the General and worn with such obvious pride.

"How much money do you make, Private Luzon?"

"Seventy-eight dollars a month, sir!"

Satisfied, the General made a smart right turn to go on down the rank.

"How much you make, sir?"

The General turned left, not nearly so smartly, and faced Luzon again, with a kind of confused look on his face. Sweat, which had begun on the Captain when the General started down the second rank, now showed clearly through his starched fatigues.

The General said, "Eleven hundred dollars a month."

"GOLLLLEEE!!!" ejected Luzon, with obvious respect in his inflection. "You got it made, sir, if you don't screw up!"

56

If I ever observed what can only be described as an electric silence, I observed it then. Absolutely nothing moved. The clouds even seemed to stop. The pitiful look on the Captain's face was absolutely heart rending. The General looked thunderstruck. Then he twitched a little. Then began to wilt a little. Then fought to suppress a grin. An involuntary snicker came from the rear of the formation. The General grinned. He couldn't help it. Then he leaned back and roared in genuine belly laughter, and I thought, "Good for him!" Control was lost. The battery, though standing in place, was anything but military. The Captain, taking his cue from the General, managed a sickly little smile like he had just swallowed a live lizard and was letting everybody know that it didn't bother him. Luzon was grinning broadly as he looked from right to left and seemed to say, "Didn't I do good! Now this is more like it!"

The General didn't inspect any more troops. He got in his car and left. And I got my ass chewed bad enough that I still remember the chewing verbatim. It's the only thing I remember verbatim about the army, and that was twenty-five years ago at the time of this painful remembering.

After the memorable stint in the army, I got serious about starting a career, so I got a job selling computers and other data processing stuff with a little outfit called IBM. I bought myself a couple of dark suits, a bunch of white shirts, two pairs of wing-tip shoes and a couple of striped ties and got after it.

They assigned me to a territory consisting of State and Local Government accounts and prospects, and I sold *a bunch* of stuff.

I mean, I won lots of awards and made some Hundred Percent Clubs, and even took my bride to the Golden Circle in Hawaii. I knew the Governor on a first name basis and was offered promotions to lots of places. It was a heady time.

Mississippi has eighty-two counties, and only one at that time, the biggest county in the state, had data processing equipment. I got to thinking that if I could sell a smaller county some equipment, I could "reference sell" other counties, and stir up about eighty serious prospects, and probably sell sixty or so of them. The only problem that would face me with sixty new accounts was to find a bank big enough to hold all of the commissions and a CPA who could figure in high enough numbers to tell me how much income tax I owed. And with all of the awards and things, selling a little county would be a cinch. Like picking cherries off a tree.

Each of the counties was run by a board of five individuals called Supervisors, and I managed to find a Supervisor in a small county who was interested. His name was Hub. He was a fine, older gentleman who was really interested in his county keeping up with the latest in technology. This county also had in its area an excellent junior college with a computer. All the county had to buy was a keypunch, a card sorter, and a small machine called a tabulator. The keypunch was to punch holes in the cards, the sorter placed the cards in the proper sequence, and the tabulator just printed what was punched in the cards. The junior college could run the serious stuff on their computer and were excited about the correct politics of helping the county (from whence most of their serious funds were obtained). Shoot, it was a natural.

Hub gained me a spot on the Board of Supervisors agenda at the next meeting. He advised me, "Now, Jim, you got to keep it *simple*. I'm talking about *real* simple. I'm talking *basic*." I said, "Yes, Sir," and prepared my presentation. It was a beautiful presentation. Imagine a stand-up, flip chart, forty-five minute presentation of how to punch holes in cards and put them in order! It was crystal clear. It was interspersed with just the appropriate number of names like the Governor's, the State Auditor's, and others of importance dropped at just the right time. It was really a mismatch. They wouldn't have a chance.

The grand moment arrived on the agenda of the next meeting of the Board, when Hub introduced me to begin the presentation. I had by this time graduated to a three-piece dark suit, and I stood out in the crowd. I expertly and smoothly unfolded my flip chart stand, assembled my charts, rolled off the perfect opening remarks, and began the powerful oratory. The thing went perfectly. They were absolutely silent and very attentive, obviously hanging onto every silver word. I was counting the money.

When the presentation was over, Hub, looking very pleased, leaned back and looked at the President of the Board in the eye.

(This was pretty difficult, because the President, a short little chubby baldheaded fellow, didn't have very big eyes.) "Well, John, what do you think?" John stretched a little and said, "Aw, you boys do whatever you think we ought to do. I quit listening to this feller about thirty minutes ago. This kind of shit makes my head hurt." The rest of the Board nodded in agreement. I looked at Hub. Hub looked at me and shrugged. I folded my tent and faded into the sunset. Far as I know this particular county has not in the ensuing twenty years installed one stick of data processing equipment. But this is the one presentation I remember best.

Ah, the good old days. Friend, you can have 'em.

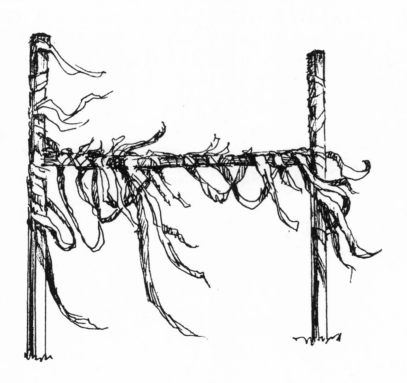

BULLS, BALLS & B B'S

A long time ago, us healthy, resourceful little country boys, though bereft of plastic toys and electronic games and such, could generally find amusement enough to keep ourselves busy. Things like bending oak boards for days between trees so that they retained their bowed shapes, waxing the outer sides of the board, then sitting in the bow and sliding down the steep, leafy sides of the wooded hollows were great fun. Fun, that is until the boy, the board, and a hickory tree on too steep a slope all married up together and various parts of the board or the boy splintered off. Most of the time no real harm was done, and if something perchance got broken, sprained, or pulled, the victim had nobody to blame but himself.

While these encounters with unyielding trees were avoided (the closer the avoidance, the better), even the encounters, if they were serious enough, were pay-offs in their own way if your peers were watching. Limping was expected. Unconsciousness, feigned or real, always generated admiring conversation from the onlookers. "Old Jimmy must have been going eighty or ninety miles an hour when he hit that oak. Lookit the bark he knocked off of it with his *head!*"

The highest pinnacle you could reach was to have something wind up in a cast. Then there was no question of the validity of the injury. The doctor said it was broke, so it must be broke. A face would show the strain of pain for days after the pain had left, especially while the prettier girls were signing the cast. Martyrdom isn't necessarily learned. I think it's natural and often useful. I still use the technique sometimes, even though I haven't broken anything or slid on a board for years.

Another creative pastime usually took place a month or so after Christmas. It had to be about that time because the bow'n'arrer Santa brought was usually down by that time to one usable arrow. The other three in the set were either broken, devoid of feathers, warped, or lost in the thick woods where a record grizzly had been missed narrowly. "I'd of killed him if I hadn't of lost that arrer I missed him with." When you were down to one arrow, you sure didn't want to lose it, because next Christmas was an eternity away. So you could only shoot it out in the pasture where the grass was short. And you had to shoot it up at a high angle so that when it came down, it stuck up and was easy to find.

Well, shooting an arrow straight up is fun for a maximum of maybe three minutes. So a twist had to be invented. In this case, another nine year old companion is required. He lies down in the

pasture face down and is not allowed to peek. You carefully
gauge the distance, windage, relative humidity and earth rotation,
and speed the arrow upward. If your calculations are right and
aim is true, the arrow will stick up very close to where he is lying.
The closer the better. "That arrer nicked my shirt!" Then, in the
absence of penetration of the body by the arrow, you exchange
places.

This game usually lasted for at least an hour or two, and
could usually be counted on to generate much conversation about
the nearness of the nearest misses. To my recollection, nobody
was ever impaled. Nor were mothers ever told of the game.

Neither of the above activities has anything to do with The
Bull. They were mentioned only to acquaint you, however briefly,
with the general bent (or warp) of a shirt-tail country kid's idea of
having fun using limited resources. But give him a resource!
Then he positively radiates in his entertainment capacity.

One resource in this tale came in the form of the magnificent
gift to me by my father of a genuine Red Ryder BB gun! Blue,
oiled steel! Genuine wood stock and forearm! Leather thong!
Crisp action! My joy was boundless. No more time for bent
boards or bow'n'arrers. The woods, the pastures, the briar patches,
the *world* took on a new appearance. I was absolute master of
every situation. In my everyday uniform of no shirt, no shoes,
blue jeans (not the stiff, heavy denims with red tabs or designer
pockets, but blowsy legged, loose crotched, big pocketed,
wonderful, flappy with the right-leg-always-rolled-up-so-you-

won't-catch-it-in-the-bicycle-chain blue jeans), and my Red Ryder BB gun, I was invincible. Birds of all kinds with the possible exception of full-grown buzzards were in mortal danger when I prowled the woods with the unerring, unquestioning faithful companion which never failed me. What with the abundance of tin cans, fence posts, trees, and other big game, the supply of BBs melted rapidly. Sometimes a whole nickel's worth would be exhausted in a day. (That was a lot of BBs then.) Since my week's allowance was a dime, serious self-imposed rationing would be implemented 'til the next Saturday when a dime would again be issued to me. The dime usually remained in my possession for ten to fifteen minutes, which was the time it took, depending on the weather, to run or bike the half-mile of gravel road from my house to Mr. Rollins' little store to buy two more nickel tubes of copper plated, shiny, perfectly round, beautiful BBs. Then the woods had to again contend with me and Red Ryder.

This cycle lasted for about a month. Red Ryder and I merged into a team. My marksmanship improved to the point where I quit worrying about whether I could hit a Prince Albert can and started concentrating on hitting the picture of Prince Albert. Then Prince Albert's head. I mean I could *shoot*!

The BB gun did have something to do with The Bull. The Bull was a Jersey, owned by our down the road neighbor, Mr. Rankin, and his domain was a small rectangular pasture of ten acres or so, which joined our place. One narrow side of the

66

pasture joined Mr. Rankin's barn and barnyard, and the other three sides were bordered by woods which came right up to the fences. The woods provided ample cover for us to slip up close to the fence and watch The Bull with awe and not a little fear. Sometimes, if we were really lucky and quiet, we could ease up close enough to actually smell the strong musky odor of him as he snuffed at the short grass and shuffled his big feet while munching and moving at his own speed and not worrying about who or what was close to him. I can remember the apprehension I felt when The Bull would suddenly throw up his big head, swing it toward me, and just *look*.

He was a classic Jersey. Huge forequarters, head, and neck, sloped back to trimmer hindquarters. He had wicked curved black horns, a curly forehead, mean little eyes which simply challenged you to even think about challenging him in any fashion, and a perpetually wet, bubbly black nose replete with a stout nose ring. He was mean. Nobody messed with The Bull. We were absolutely forbidden by parents to set even one foot inside The Bull's pasture. So we didn't do it often. If The Bull was up close to the barn, sometimes a dare would send one of us scampering across the pasture at the other end. If The Bull was located a little closer, a double dare might work, but it took a double *dog* dare to get anybody in that pasture when The Bull was relatively close. The double dog dares accepted sometimes resulted in a chase, and everybody held his breath until the chasee dived to safety through the barbed wire into the woods. The Bull always stopped at the fence. We never understood why, because his huge bulk could have ripped wire, posts, staples, and all down if he had decided to accomplish same. He must have had a bad experience with fences as a calf or something, because he always stopped short and put on a show. He would snort, paw the ground, throwing grass and dirt over his massive shoulders and back, and toss those lethal horns seeming to double *double* dog dare the chasee to give him one more chance. That awesome display generally put the damper on anybody accepting another double dog dare for a few days until the effect wore off.

The preacher in his sermons sometimes would use the term "So and So sprang from the loins of So and So." Little country boys living close to nature had a general idea of how that kind of thing occurred. What with the observations of the animals, and whispered conversations on the school playground, the idea gained credence, but the formal anatomical terms got a little garbled. We knew from whence things sprang, so the formal terms for them became loins. The Bull's loins hung down about eighteen inches. Like everything else about him, these twin globes were huge. We admired them.

It was on a summer's afternoon that our relationship with The Bull completely changed. I happened to be sitting very still by a tree close to The Bull's pasture fence, armed with Red Ryder, and probably concentrating on the woods' sights and sounds as I loved to do. My attention was interrupted by a munching, snuffling sound behind me, and I slowly, carefully turned my head toward the sound. It was The Bull, fifty or so feet away in his pasture, shuffling along nuzzling the short grass and blissfully unaware that anyone was within a half mile of him. I thought of pinging him in the shoulder or side with a BB, just for the hell of it, and beating a hasty retreat. Somehow that just didn't seem sporting. His massive bulk produced such a huge target that the challenge wasn't there. Then I focused on the loins. Challenging, but attainable. Reaction undiscovered. Experiment irresistible. I eased Red Ryder to my shoulder, took careful aim at the left one, and sent the BB on its way. The Bull's life changed. He saw me the moment I pulled the trigger, so his association of the cause with the effect was accurate. The effect that first time never varied in the ensuing times over the months which followed. At the sound of the BB gun's expulsion of air which sent the BB winging, The Bull's head would swing up in reaction. The invariable little cloud of dust would puff out around the loins when the BB smacked home. A strangled bellow-roar would shatter the air and The Bull would take a gigantic leap in whichever direction he happened to be headed at the time. He always hit the ground running full tilt with his great hooves thundering a rapid tattoo until he was confronted by the fence. Then he'd stop and swing his massive head, looking not for someone to charge, but for someone to put the maximum distance between himself and.

I began to swagger. The situation had reversed. After several such encounters, I began to stalk The Bull. I could step in the pasture and The Bull would go to the other end. His attitude had become much more civilized. He may have had murder on his mind, but his loins had other thoughts, and they invariably won that internal argument.

We moved away shortly after this situation had developed. I'm sure that in the ensuing years The Bull has died. I remember my father assuring me as he buried our old setter bird dog, Buddy, whom I loved and was loudly and tearfully mourning, that good animals can also go to Heaven. If this is true, and if by some foul-up in the great computer in the sky The Bull is up there, when my time comes I want to be sure of a couple of things before I take up residence. Either the angels have him penned behind barbed wire, or I need to be issued the Heavenly facsimile of a Red Ryder BB gun. Otherwise, I'm not sure I want to go.

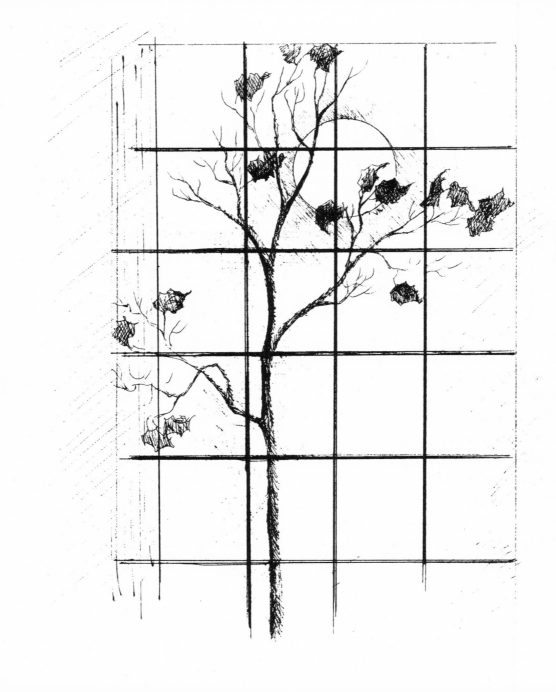

THINGS THAT GO
BUMP IN THE NIGHT

Imagination is a wonderful thing. It works best in the dark. The darker the better.

When you can't see something, you can make it as beautiful or as ugly or as big or as little or as scary or as peaceful as you want it to be. That's what my papa told me once when I woke suddenly from a sound sleep and was sure that a grizzly was snuffing around my bed one particularly dark night. Turned out that when he responded to my fire alarm-sized scream for help, it was my little brother doing the snuffing in his sleep, and the reason it sounded so close was that we shared a double bed. It was sort of disappointing that it was my little brother and not a grizzly. I would have just as soon faced a grizzly as to put up with all of his strange noises and kicks as he slept after a big supper of smoked sausage and eggs and biscuits. Besides, he had the unique capability of pooting in his sleep. I had never heard of an enraged grizzly pooting. I guess if an enraged grizzly did poot, you would be up and running and not have to lie there in the dark wondering if you ought to fan the covers and get it over with in a hurry or just let everything rot around you slowly. Little brothers are a pain in the ass.

While I realize that the comforting words my papa gave me that night are true ninety-nine percent of the time, the remaining one percent of the possibilities gets awful swollen when it's *really* dark. Let me give you a few examples.

The house always sounds different when my wife and the kids aren't there. Quiet as a tomb. (I wonder why I always say that. I never even been in a tomb. How the hell should I know how quiet a tomb is? May be a party going on in there for all I know. Especially in those concreted-up ones.)

I don't remember what the occasion was that prompted Perry to take the young'uns to her folks' house in Laurel one week, but it left me in hated isolation, especially at night. It wasn't that I was scared. It was just so damned *quiet*.

One of the nights they were gone that week, I woke up in the predawn hours, very alert. I didn't open my eyes at first. Just listened. I heard every small rustle and squeak, and none of them sounded like natural things. I thought to myself, "Now, you're a grown, healthy, strong man. What is this nonsense?" So I opened my eyes and unmistakably saw a form pass a few feet beyond the foot of my bed. It was pretty dark, but not so dark that I couldn't make out shapes and forms. And this form was real. And moving. Sort of swaying back and forth. I knew it was looking at me. I don't know if my first reaction was fear or anger, but the anger took over pretty quick. The son of a bitch was in my house. Uninvited. I was incensed. So I came exploding out of the bed trailing sheets and covers and hit it as hard as I ever hit anything or anybody. I mean I *unloaded*. The noise created was indescribable. Things broke, rattled, and fluttered. And I'd never hit anything that felt exactly like that thing did.

What it was, was a sliding closet door. See, there was a window by the head of my bed. And the moon was bright. And there was a little sycamore tree in the yard between my window and the moon. And a light wind was blowing the little sycamore tree back and forth. And the little sycamore's big shadow was projected through my window onto the sliding closet door. All I can say is that the shadow damn sure didn't look like a little sycamore tree. Anyway, the short of it is that I busted a hole in the closet door and knocked it off its railing. When it got all tangled up with the hanging clothes, the clothes fluttered and the coat hangers rattled. Pretty simple stuff if your adrenaline level isn't bumping the top of your head. But if it's dark, and you're charged up for battle, all that racket simply spurs you on.

I mauled the clothes for a minute before I found the light switch and everything cleared up. I was embarrassed for myself. I had a split middle knuckle and my arm hurt all the way up to my elbow, and the poor, innocent closet door was history. I explained to Perry when she returned that I had gotten that new closet door because I was finally fed up with having to rassle and jerk around on the old one when it stuck on those railings. She had been after me for a while to fix it anyway. The new one solved the problem.

One year I had a college roommate named "Snake." That wasn't his real name, of course, but most folks didn't know what his real name was. Most of them knew the name Snake, though. Because in those days, Snake was probably the nastiest person we knew. He was a kind, generous, loveable, easy-tempered soul, but he was nasty. He used to throw his dirty clothes in a pile on the closet floor, and when he ran out of clothes in his chest of drawers or hanging in the closet, he would rummage around in the pile to find the ones least offensive and wear them for a day or two. Then he'd repeat the process the next day. This might go on for a month until he finally would go home and take the pile to be washed. Being closed up in a room with him was something you remembered. I used to smoke pretty heavy when we were together.

I hit the end of my rope with him one afternoon when for some reason, his bed got my attention. The background color of his sheets was nondescript. The foreground color was distinct. A sort of abstract filthy. Everywhere there was a wrinkle, there was a black line.

I said, "Snake, you're a friend of mine. But I'm going to the library and study for a little while, and when I get back, if those sheets aren't off that bed, I'm either going to throw them out of this second-story window or burn them. This kind of living ain't healthy." He agreed, and I left. I came back a couple of hours later and Snake was gone. The sheets weren't. I held my breath, stripped them off, and flung them out the window, then settled back to wait for him to come in. I was sure that he would get pretty stirred up about my throwing his stuff away, but I was about ready for some kind of a showdown.

He finally wandered in, looked at the bed, didn't say a word, gathered up his blanket and bedspread, put them back on the bed, and slept between them and the bare mattress for the rest of the semester. What happened to those sheets remains a mystery. We never saw them again.

Anyway, Snake had an experience similar to my sliding closet door encounter. He and a friend of his went on a hunting trip one time and spent a couple of nights in an old abandoned shack in the woods. According to him, the weather was drizzly, cold, and generally miserable. Just right for hunting. But the nights were black. They had one little battery powered hand lantern they used for lighting the whole shack, but that was enough to allow them to function. Functioning meant opening a can of vienna sausages or sardines and a package of crackers and finding the whiskey, of which they partook too much on the last night they were there.

They had wisely decided not to light a fire in the rickety old fireplace, since the old tinderbox of a cabin might have burned down around their ears if a stray spark had popped out while they were asleep. So they had gathered up some corrugated boxes found in the cabin, flattened them out, and placed them under their sleeping bags for cushioning and additional insulation, turned out the lantern, and sank into a stupor.

In the middle of the night, Snake awoke to the most horrifying sound he had ever heard. Said it was an ear-piercing SCREEEEEEE......SCREEEEEEE....SCREEEESCREEEESCREEEE ...SCREEEEE!!! Then a stop and then SCREEEEEing again. Not over a couple of feet from his head, which had already begun to throb with the promise of a real beauty of a hangover later. It was obvious to him that something as awful as could be imagined had done away with his friend in an incredibly heinous way and was preparing to dispatch him in the same blood-curdling manner. He opted in that critical instant to fight for his life. He mentally reconstructed the last lighted scene he could remember before sleep and alcohol had robbed him of wakefulness, and pictured where his shotgun and the lantern had been. Then, with one swift movement, he sprang from his sleeping bag, screaming like a banshee to immobilize his adversary, grabbed his gun and the lantern, and turned the full light on the noise. Now that's what *he* said. I have a mental picture of him fumbling with the zipper on the sleeping bag, groping for the gun and the lantern, and trying to figure out how to turn the thing on. I have no doubt about the screaming.

The light revealed his drunk friend sitting cross-legged with a piece of corrugated cardboard on his lap, sawing a strip of it off with a dull pocketknife. Hence the SCREEEEEEEEEing noise. His drunk friend said, "I'm cold! And I'm going to start a fire!"

blinking into the direct beam of the lantern. "What's the matter with you, anyway, hollering like that? You scared the hell out of me!"

Snake, even-tempered as he was, called his friend some terrible things, and then went outside and threw up the remainder of the sardines and whiskey. Which probably considerably diminished the effects of the morning-after syndrome. He didn't remember if he had actually pointed the gun at his friend when he switched the lantern on, but it really didn't make any difference. He had, as all good hunters do, unloaded it before he brought it indoors.

You know, the more I think about it, it really doesn't have to be dark for imagination to conjure up unpleasant things if the conditions are right.

I've got a couple of old compadres, who happen to be twins, one named Bones, and the other named Grezzer. I've spent many a memorable time with these two, and, the Good Lord willing, I'll spend some more. One of these times might illustrate the imagination-in-the-daytime point.

Every year a bunch of the old college fraternity brothers get together for a fishing trip at the Chandeleur Islands, about forty miles out in the Gulf of Mexico, due south of Gulfport. The twins are always in the bunch. Bones, the oldest of the two by a couple of minutes, has never pretended to be a John Wayne-type hero. Matter of fact, he accepts the fact that he is a little skittish when the matter of his personal safety is threatened. Now, that is not to be interpreted as a derogatory statement about Bones. It's just that he may be counted on to be a little less inclined than most of the rest of us to place himself in harm's way. Which, truth be known, probably makes him smarter than the rest of us.

On one of the fishing trips, the speckled trout weren't cooperating enough to suit us where we had anchored the big sleeping boats, so Bones, Grezzer, and I decided to take one of the smaller skiffs over to a nearby smaller island and see if we could have better luck. We decided to spread out and wade the shallows, separated from each other by maybe five or six hundred yards. We let Bones out of the skiff first, then I dropped off Grezzer next, and drove the skiff on further down the beach before I anchored, got out, and waded. I don't remember whether we caught any fish, but when it came time to head back for the big boats, I picked up Grezzer first and we made for Bones' location. We could see him standing in knee-deep water casting his lure and looking right and left as he retrieved, evidently making sure that no sharks or other unlovely things might be in his vicinity.

We didn't want to beach the heavy skiff, so we stopped the boat forty or fifty feet out from Bones' position and told him to come on out to us. We didn't know that a pretty deep cut, or place where the water deepened, was between us and Bones. He began the slow wade to the skiff. The water rose to his thighs, waist, shoulders, and finally about twenty feet from the boat, he was in water considerably over his head. He was holding his rod above his head with one hand and stroking with the other, roundly cussing us for not knowing anything about the beach and making him swim so far. Grezzer, having had enough of his brother's verbal abuse, gave Bones enough time to get in the middle of the cut and said in a forced, matter-of-fact manner, "Bones, just keep a steady, even stroke, and for God's sake, *don't look behind you.*"

Bones took his brother's advice. He did not look behind him, and his stroke was steady and even. Sort of like an eggbeater. I would not have believed that salt water could be whipped to a lather that creamy. He beat that imaginary, toothy monster to the skiff, and when he had time to observe me and Grezzer collapsed in mirth on the bottom of the skiff, he let it be known that we both were in danger of having the hell beat out of us. Fortunately for me and Grezzer, brotherhood, both blood and fraternity, saved us.

I'm sure that you have had similar experiences. And when you stop to think about them, you get a little sheepish and vow, as I have, to not let little, natural things make your imagination run wild again. It's ridiculous to do so. As I write this, I'm alone, and it's plenty dark outside. And it's not bothering me a bit. And....

What the hell was that noise?

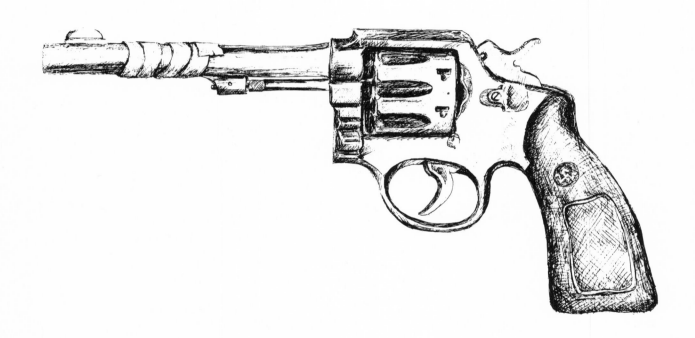

WHAT'S IN A NAME?

His name is Stud. At first glance, the name seems ludicrous. He wears pretty thick glasses, is bordering on obesity, with a belly that hangs generously over his belt, has a complete bridge to compensate for the middle four missing upper front teeth, talks and laughs in almost a falsetto, is pretty scarred up as a result of a bad car accident, and in general appearance, ain't nothing to write home about. Appearances, as the saying goes, are deceiving.

To use his own words, he's "two hundred and forty pounds of walking, stomping hell, master of all men, God's gift to women, and the answer to a teenager's prayer." And the disturbing thing is, he *believes* it! He'll "fight a buzz saw and give it a 250 rpm head start," again to use his own words. And I've seen him in action enough times to where I believe that!

When it comes to servicing females, he believes in equal opportunity for everyone, like the Constitution says, and was far ahead of his time in putting that idea into practice. Race, creed, or ethnic origin means nothing to him, and he is equally impervious to deformities, blindness, deafness, age, intellect, political persuasion, denomination, height, weight, baldness, cellulite, talent, or career aspirations. Stud don't cull nothing. (His words, again.) He handles feminists, shrews, angels, intellectuals, and air heads with equal aplomb, and it beats the hell out of me how he does it.

He plays poker and shoots craps with a vengeance, will drink any potion containing alcohol (including home-grown stuff which, according to the maker of one particular batch with which I used to be familiar, could be cut down for human consumption only by something like kerosene), and will absolutely gut an automobile in thirty-five thousand miles or less.

I've used the present tense in describing him, though I haven't seen him in twenty years. That's the way he was, and unless he's had a road to Damascus experience in that time, I'd bet he hasn't changed a bit. Leopard's spots and all that.

I first met Stud when I was a freshman in college. I was eighteen, my neck had swelled up as a result of rising sap, virginity had recently fled, my nose and knuckles stayed pretty skinned up, since my philosophy was that a good, clean fight could solve an argument much more quickly and decisively than long, verbal battles requiring a fairly extensive vocabulary which I didn't have, and I was a sort of self-proclaimed "bad ass." So Stud and I hit it off immediately. Difference was, he had spent four years in the Air Force before coming to Ole Miss, and was much more worldly than I. He was a constant source of "war stories" involving first person experiences with folks who would make the Damon Runyan characters seem like a model Sunday School class. I developed a case of hero worship.

We had both pledged Sigma Nu, so the comradery was strengthened even more, and together we managed to bring the pledge class grade point average down considerably. I was enrolled in pre-med the first semester, during which a chemistry class under a professor named C. N. (Cyanide) Jones convinced me that I did not belong in that austere group. Stud, a little more realistic concerning his career pursuits and level of intellect, had chosen a business administration curriculum, which I also finally chose after stints in the aforementioned pre-med, then liberal arts, then economics, then petroleum engineering.

The only class we had together was a freshman English composition class taught by an ancient female PhD. She was a tough old spinster: short, squat, and slightly stooped, with her gray hair always pulled back severely into a bun at the nape of her short neck. Thick bifocals protected her watery eyes, which glared out of a face like four miles of washed out road. I never really got close enough to her to tell for sure, but with her looks and disposition, I could imagine festoons of green meat hanging out of her ears. I managed a C in the course and Stud made a D. He said he had trouble concentrating in class because he was constantly planning ways to get her in the sack. Jesus. I still quake at that thought. I started not to tell you about this, but I figured you needed some evidence of what I meant earlier when I said that Stud was non-discriminatory.

Stud always shaved with a straight razor. He claimed that when you shaved with a straight razor, you paid more attention to what you were doing instead of using a safety razor like you were "raking leaves," and actually cut yourself less often. Nobody argued with him on that point, but this area was one in which he had no converts.

I got a chance to shave *him* with it once. Stud had been invited to a sorority formal on campus. I was surprised at this, because his reputation was pretty well known, and he had a few problems getting dates when he initiated the action, let alone being asked out by a real, live coed. And the one who asked him to this particular party was a beauty. I guess she had decided that he possibly had been the victim of vicious gossip, and she would rectify this gross error and restore him to respectability. Besides, they would be on a double date with one of her sorority sisters and her tried-and-true boyfriend.

Stud started getting ready for the party at 'round 11 a.m. The dance started at 8 p.m. I got to the dorm at around 3 that afternoon, and Stud was well on his way to getting ready. The fifth of bourbon on his chest of drawers had had some real damage done to it, and he was in fine spirits. A few onlookers had helped him start to get dressed so that he would not be late, and by the time I entered the scene, he had on his tux pants and shirt and suspenders. He was barefooted and had not shaved. I

86

suggested that these two items should be tended to. He said the shoes were the last thing he was going to put on just before leaving because one of us clumsy bastards would probably step on them and mess up the spit shine. He admitted that he had forgotten to shave, and, since he was just a little shaky, that I should perform the honors.

Now, I'd never shaved anything, including myself, with a straight razor. But I figured that it was infinitely better to practice on him than me. However, I did advise him to take that crisp white tux shirt off before we began just in case a tiny mistake was made. He looked me straight in the eye and said, "It took me thirty minutes to get all them little things fixed in the front and these cuffs wadded up so that the holes matched for the cuff links, and I ain't going through that again. Besides, you're going to be *real* careful and not cut me, aren't you?", with his nose about a quarter inch from mine. I said yes.

It was like trying to cut barbed wire with a butter knife. I'd scrape a little spot, lather it back up and scrape it again. About an hour later, I was through. He wasn't shaved too good, but I was through. There were some clean spots, and some which looked like they hadn't been touched, but I figured that when you took an average, it was O.K. He had been touching the bourbon throughout it all, and when I announced it was over, he looked in the mirror, swiped his hand over his fat jowls, smiled and said it was just right. Slapped a double handful of shaving lotion on, cringed a little, and allowed as how he probably needed to sharpen the razor before the next time. I said it wouldn't hurt, and had a little touch of bourbon myself.

Well, the appointed time finally came, and we sent a wobbly Prince Charming on his way, and settled down to a poker game, since it was Friday night, and we didn't have classes on Saturday in those days. About midnight, Prince Charming showed back up, bloody as a stuck hog. I mean, he looked *bad*. There were rivulets of blood, fresh and dried, all down his face and neck, and the once snowy shirtfront was a mess. And Stud was genuinely confused. Seemed that after the dance, he had decided not to let a backseat situation go to waste, and had made his move. Which was to pin her under his bulk and whisper sweet nothings like, "They ain't gonna hear us," and "How do these damn hooks work?" He said she was saying things like "Get offa me" and "Stop it, Stud," but she wasn't saying it loud enough to be really persuasive, and she was wiggling, which he took as another positive sign. Turned out, however, that the wiggling accomplished its mission, which was to free an arm enough to reach her foot and grab a spiked high-heeled shoe, with which she banged on his head a few times, hence a scalp wound, hence the blood. This really upset Stud, who backed off and sulked in his corner, and was damned if he was going to pay her any more attention, no matter what good manners dictated. He allowed as how some women were hard as hell to figure. What really hurt his feelings and puzzled him, however, was that she never asked him out again. I offered no suggestions.

There was a little game in those days that we used to play on selected freshmen. Most of us experienced types had it pulled on us in high school, or at least we had heard about it. But it was amazing to me the number of freshmen who were ignorant about it. Most college freshmen, you see, are semi-eager and semi-reluctant at the same time to participate in illicit functions either to prove their manhood or to be a member of the group. So most of them were ripe for a little adventure, especially if a group was involved.

We would sit around in a bull session with the picked freshman and topics would range on all kinds of subjects. Then somebody would ask in a kind of knowing way what we thought Bernice might be up to tonight. It would come out in the conversation that Bernice was a good looking girl who lived with her father way out in the country and whose morals would make an alley cat blush.

Her father worked for the railroad, which kept a strict schedule as railroads do, and was never home before 11:30 at night. This left poor Bernice alone with nothing to do between the time she got home from work until her father got home. And she always welcomed company, and groups were her favorite way to entertain.

Both she and her father were fictitious, of course, but she came very much to life and her talents were legend in these conversations. A suggestion would be made that, hell, we might as well go on over to see her tonight, and folks would begin to get ready to go. If the freshman decided to go with us, somebody would beg off going because he needed to study or some such nonsense, and leave right then. He would race to the fraternity house, gather up two or three others, get a shotgun, and head for an old abandoned shack down a gravel road way out in the country.

The group with the freshman would lag around getting coats, visiting the john, etc., to give the shotgun group a good head start; then amidst much anticipation, excited conversation, and much slapping the freshman on the back to ensure that no second thoughts were beginning to creep in, the group would head for Bernice's.

When the courting group arrived at the house, it would park the car a reasonable distance away and begin to walk across the front yard to the front porch. When they would get about midway across the yard, a form would appear in the dark nightly shadows of the front porch and holler, "So *you're* the trash that's been up here getting at my daughter," and the shotgun would blast. One of the courting group would always grab his belly and scream something like "I'm hit! For God's sake, don't leave me!" fall to the ground, and the group would scatter.

Sometimes the freshman could not be found for days. I've seen them run through barbed wire fences, sail off into kudzu covered gullies, and one ran smack into a pine tree, backed off and ran into the same tree two more times before he finally figured out how to get around it. Sheer panic lends wings to feet, and they generally ran far enough to get lost in the dark. The group would get back in the cars after much conversation about the speed and enthusiasm with which the freshman had vacated the premises and go on back to the campus, leaving the freshman to his own designs.

One night we had just such a bull session with a targeted freshman. Stud was also in the group. The freshman decided that he didn't want to go, and the whole thing sort of simmered down. Then Stud said, "What are we waiting for? Let's go!" I was shocked. Stud didn't know! My God, what an opportunity!

Well, things moved right along according to plan, and when we got halfway across the yard, the form appeared, the gun went off, and I yelled, grabbed my belly, and dropped down by an old log which was lying in the yard. Stud came by me like a freight train. I poured it on and screamed, "Stud, *please* don't leave me! I'm shot!" He looked over, saw who it was, changed directions, and flopped over behind the log. "I ain't gonna leave you," he said. Then he reached under his coat and pulled out a pistol that, I swear, looked like it was three feet long. I distinctly remember that it had white adhesive tape wrapped around the barrel for some unknown reason.

Stud raised up over the log and sent a shot whistling through one of the windows and I heard the bullet rattle off the back wall. I also heard some conversation from the house. "Some son of a bitch is shooting back!"

"Why?"

"How the hell do I know? Get down!"

"What do we do now?"

"I don't know, goddammit, get down *lower*!"

"I can't. My shirt buttons are in the way!"

Stud raised up and blasted away again, causing more conversation and scurrying around in the house. He looked over at me and said, "How bad are you hurt?"

Well now, as you can see, I've got me a real problem. I've got a few fraternity brothers in the house in danger of getting shot at, and I've got two hundred and forty pounds of walking, stomping hell, even without a pistol, who is owed a confession. Conscience is nagged concerning the former, and physical health is potentially endangered by the latter. I'm telling you, the wheels were turning.

"I said are you hurt bad?"

"Naw."

"Can you make it to the car?"

"Stud, uh, we need to talk."

"For God's sake, not now. We're in a crisis. Can't you see that?"

"It really ain't that bad."

"Look, don't pull that hero crap right now. There's a shotgun pointed at us, and that tends to make me nervous as hell. I don't want to shoot him, but I'm not sure we can make it back across that open yard."

"I really don't think they'll shoot at us."

"*They?* How many of them did you see?"

"Three, I think."

"Damn! It's worse than I thought. That settles it. We'll just have to shoot it out."

"Hey, Stud, what if I have a way to get us out without a scratch, guaranteed, and make you laugh at the same time?"

"Boy, you must've lost a lot of blood. I've heard that the brain don't function too good without enough blood."

I took a deep breath and explained, talking very fast and watching the pistol. Stud thought for a minute, and a slow grin spread over his ample face.

"You mean we've got old Gil and two more of our boys holed up in that house?"

"Yep. And they don't know whether to shit or go blind with you shooting back. Why don't you shoot again at the tin roof and then listen real close."

He did, and the sound of the bullet slamming into the old loose tin was awful. We heard a lot of scurrying around and what sounded like the old rattly-assed back screen door slam shut as the occupants sailed out, headed for the kudzu covered gullies. He shot two more times into the tin roof to make sure the running didn't stop, and we strolled to the car, cranked up and headed for the campus. The subject of the trick on him didn't come up, but he was sure tickled over the plight of the boys who were probably still hunkered down in the kudzu. And that suited the hell out of me.

There were many more escapades. Too many to go into here. But the point is, I wonder if, having read about the effect of a name on folks by psychologists of note, he had been called Alfonse or Mortimer, given his physical traits, he would have been the same person.

I'm glad he wasn't called Alfonse or Mortimer. I'm glad they called him Stud.

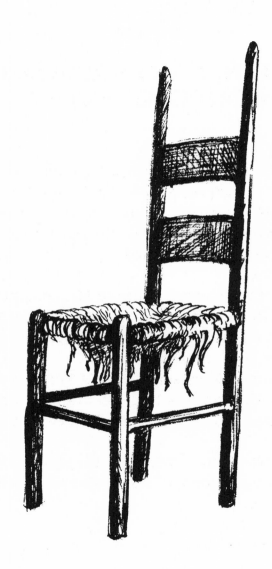

CAT, CABIN, CAUTERIZATION
AND CONFLAGRATION

A hole in a pair of overhauls...overhauls?...overalls... *overhauls*...still sounds right...can, under a given set of circumstances, cause awful events to occur. I heard a story once about a hole in a pair of overhauls which, combined with just such a set of circumstances, caused a perfectly good dwelling to be burned to the ground.

A college friend of mine came from the Mississippi Delta. In those days, Ole Miss students from the Delta just lived different. Always seemed to have bigger farms, raise bigger crops, drive bigger cars, have bigger bank accounts, and for sure, seemed to tell bigger stories than ordinary Mississippi folks. This friend of mine (name of Denman) was the son of a large plantation owner. (I mean the plantation was large. The owner, Denman's father, as I recall, was normal size.)

There were several families living on the plantation who either worked for his father directly or who sharecropped parts of the place. One of the families had a big kid who sort of stood out from the other kids because everything about him was big, loose, or gangling. Big hands, big feet, big ears, big grin, long arms, long legs, loose walk, etc. They called him Teebie.

After the harvest, when the crop money came in, Teebie and all the rest of the boys usually got a new pair of overhauls to replace last year's pair. The system worked pretty well, since the new, stiff denim was pretty thick and warm during the winter and by spring, they had become faded, loose and comfortable for wear in hot weather. There might be a few rips or tears evident, but for sure there was one place in the overhauls where they had been worn almost beyond repair. What with activities such as sliding down bannisters, sliding down trees, or climbing over barbed wire fences, the crotch was non-existent. This hole was almost never repaired for a couple of reasons. First, the hole was not apparent, and second, when the top button on the sides was left unbuttoned, the air could circulate up through the crotch and around the sides making every breeze, however slight, a welcome relief from the oppressive heat of the summer.

Saturday nights, weather permitting, the grown-ups would gather at one of the cabins. The furniture would be hauled out into the yard to make room for dancing or crap games, mason jars containing the local variety of popskull would be passed around, and a party would ensue into the late hours.

One such night, Teebie decided that he would inspect the goings-on at close range, and slipped up to the cabin where the party was in full blast. He was immediately discovered and banished to an empty room where he was told to wait until the party was over so that he could accompany his parents back to their own cabin since it was too late for him to negotiate the distance alone. It was early spring and still chilly, so a fire had been started in the fireplace of the empty room. Teebie was instructed by his papa in no uncertain terms to sit in front of that fire until time to go unless he wanted an extra measure of what he knew he was going to get when he got home for coming to the party uninvited in the first place. A cane bottomed chair was hauled in from the yard for the sitting. Problem was, the cane bottom had a pretty big hole in it. When Teebie sat in the chair, the hole in the chair bottom matched up with the hole in the crotch of the overhauls, and part of Teebie, long, loose, and gangling like the rest of him, swung free through the holes, unbeknownst to Teebie. His legs, though long for his age, still were short enough to allow his feet to dangle an inch or two from the floor. So he was loose and dangling all over, which suited Teebie.

Another uninvited guest, ignored by everyone at the festivities, nonchalantly wandered through the activities of the party room and squeezed through the door to the room where Teebie was obediently sitting, intently watching the fire and pondering his imminent punishment for crashing the party. The new guest was the cabin owner's big, tiger-striped, battle-scarred, iron-jawed tomcat. Once in Teebie's room, he sauntered on silent

feet over to the chair where he arched his back and rubbed against a back chair leg, still unnoticed by the morbid Teebie. The cat (name of Tom) happened to look up and notice a foreign object or set of objects dangling just out of reach.

Now this cat was no different from most other cats in that his curiosity just seemed to be an inherent part of his personality. The cat tentatively reached up with one paw and patted the object of his curiosity, and when things swung, he reared up on both hind legs, unsheathed his claws, and latched on. Teebie's attention was immediate. The total shock, fear, and uncertainty immobilized him for a split second, which was enough time for the cat to get a firm hold, and a split second later, Teebie grasped the situation, and attempted to escape. But basic laws of physics, you see, were stacked against him in almost every way you can imagine. When he lurched straight up, the old law of bigger things can't fit through smaller holes applied because the cat was bigger than the hole in the chair, and the cat wouldn't turn loose. When he bent over forward to try and reach the cat, his backside raised up in the opposite reaction you've heard about, and the weight of the cat only added to his misery. Teebie's legs couldn't reach the floor, and his arms weren't long enough the reach the cat. The loud screams and strange noises he made weren't sufficiently loud to overcome the sound of merriment in the party room. With all these laws working against him, his options were rapidly running out. Meanwhile, the cat was having a ball. (I'm sorry.) All this activity and excitement merely spurred old Tom on to harder battle.

Teebie finally took the only course open to him as he saw it. He extended both arms between his knees, waggled his fingers a couple of inches above the floor, and began to wail, "HERE, KITTY, KITTY, KITTY! HEEEEEEERE, KITTY, KITTY, KITTY!!!"

After several such pleading solicitations, the cat's attention abandoned the non-combative objects, and, expecting his usual loving rewards for responding to previous similar though less enthusiastic requests from humans, turned loose his hold and nosed up to the waggling fingers. The waggling fingers weren't friendly. With one sweeping motion, Teebie snatched the cat by the head and flung him with no thought of the direction of the cat's trajectory or safety, and ran screaming through the party. The cat landed in the fireplace and immediately realized that he was in the wrong place. He sailed out singed but unhurt, scattering burning logs and live coals and left for more friendly surroundings.

Teebie was doing some scattering of his own as dice, money, whiskey, and grownups in the party room were dispersed by the force of his entry and exit. The adults clattered out of the cabin in an effort to catch the flying Teebie, who had heard the cat scream as he hit the fire, and who had visions of the cat following right behind him, and who was in no mood to be caught.

Well, the burning logs, of course, caught the cabin on fire, and by the time the grownups had abandoned the chase after the uncatchable Teebie, the cabin was lost. A new cabin was raised in a matter of days, and the occupant family was pleased. The only casualty was the chair, and as the occupants put it, they'd trade a new house for an old cane bottomed chair any day. Besides, the chair bottom had had a hole in it anyway.

Teebie, as it turned out, didn't get the punishment he was expecting, and after a few days, he even lost the strange, spraddle-legged gait he had necessarily acquired. The cat's singed hair grew back. Denman thought that maybe this particular pair of overhauls' crotch had been sewed up. I'd bet he was right.

PAIN AIN'T FUNNY

Some people laugh at other people's pain. Or at least if not at the pain itself, at the conditions caused by the pain. Now, I know that a statement like that may frost your tail feathers and set you thinking about a cruel, inhumane monster gloating over a cowering victim and dousing him with slobber while emitting a rasping, gleeful, ungodly guffaw in response to the writhings and whimpers describing the pain being inflicted on the poor unfortunate. I ain't talking about that kind of people.

I'm talking about people you know. People you shake hands with or pray with or hug. You probably even do it yourself. You may doubt that, but I'd bet it's so.

I have a friend named Ike. He stands about six foot five in his socks and fluctuates between two hundred fifty and two hundred seventy-five pounds. One morning Ike was brushing his teeth, and while bending over the sink, he sneezed. A slipped disk resulted, and put him out of commission for weeks.

I'm familiar with the pain of back trouble. There is absolutely no way to describe it. If you've had it, you know what I mean. I'm told that the bigger you are, the worse it hurts because of all the weight grinding down on the bad spot. So I cringe when I think of what Ike went through.

For the benefit of the ignorant, I will ease through the scenario of a temporary back problem a week or so after the initial onset. You've become sick of the bed pan and other unlovely trappings necessary for you to obey the stern instructions of the orthopedist, which is to stay in bed and keep the pressure off. You grit your teeth and say to yourself, "I'm going to the bathroom, come hell or high water, and me and that bedpan are getting a *divorce!*"

You're lying on your back and you very tentatively ease one leg over the side of the bed, gingerly feeling for the floor with your toes, knowing that at any second the searing, indescribable pain will inevitably hit. And it does. So you flop over onto the floor and writhe about for a few seconds, hopefully winding up on your hands and knees, which is part of the plan. Then you start the journey to the bathroom, crawling like an infant. When you get to the bathroom, of course, you are beset with a whole new set of logistical problems, and you find out immediately that the toilet paper holder is not strong enough to hold your weight as you reach for something to help you hoist yourself up on the throne. Neither is the towel holder. We'll skip the rest of the scene.

When the deed is done, and it's time to return to the bed, you reverse the process and crawl back. Here is where we pick up again with Ike.

He'd gone through the above scenario, and was midway across the bedroom floor on his quadrupedal way back to the bed. His wife, Beverly, who is one of the sweetest people in the world, happened to walk in and spied Ike scuffling along on his hands and knees. The scene, according to her, was ludicrous. The very idea of a two hundred and seventy pound grown man crawling like that rocked her back a bit, and she started to snicker, then giggle, then get plumb uncontrollable. Ike, of course, was looking for pity, not ridicule, and stopped dead in all four tracks. He looked up at her with sagging St. Bernard eyes from which tears of anger, frustration, and pain were rolling and said, "Woman, *if* I could get up from here, I'd make you pay for that," which sent additional peals of throaty, helpless laughter directed at the ceiling.

Now, there's not a mean bone in Beverly's body. And she loves Ike and she knows that Ike loves her. And she certainly didn't relish the fact that Ike was in pain. So how come she laughed? Answer me that. But before you condemn her too much, consider another incident involving my favorite uncle.

Uncle Johnny was, among other things, a policeman. His trusted, constant partner was a fellow named "Hot." I don't recall what his real name was, but I remember Hot. They were not only partners on the police force, but they were very close friends who admired each other's personal and professional traits. I can remember Uncle Johnny telling me when I was knee high to a duck, with genuine admiration in his voice, that Hot was the only man he ever saw who could keep a tin can rolling on the ground by shooting it with a Tommygun. That kind of skill, coupled with instincts and actions, which were almost identical in both of them, created a closeness which was akin to brotherhood. This closeness extended to their families. Hot's wife Carrie and my Aunt Alice were also best of friends, as wives of men in dangerous occupations are prone to be, and socials including both families were held often. So they were true, blue, if-you-even-touch-him-in-anger-be-prepared-to-fight-me-too friends.

One fine day, Uncle Johnny and Hot were cruising around town in their police car. My uncle was aware that Hot wasn't his usual ebullient self, but he figured that if Hot wanted to talk about whatever was wrong, he would eventually get around to it without anyone having to invade his privacy with questions. So, all day long they cruised around with a minimum of conversation, and Uncle Johnny became more and more concerned. Finally, about the end of their shift, Hot raised up one side of his bottom, then the other, and groaned, "These damn hem'roids are killin' me."

Uncle Johnny, relieved finally to find out that the problem wasn't as serious as problems at home or cancer or any other of the awful things that he had conjured up in his mind all day, offered, "Why don't you just go to a doctor and have them cut out?" Hot said, "Naw. If it feels this bad riding around in this rattly-assed, no-shocked, hard-seated jalopy, can you imagine how it would feel if they were cut on? I think I'll just leave 'em alone and maybe they'll turn into a callous."

Concerned about his friend's discomfort, Uncle Johnny thought for a minute and said, "Now, Hot, that just ain't smart. You really ought to do *something*. Fella was telling me just the other day that he had had a fair case of hem'roids and went to that Indian doctor who lives outside of town. Said that old Indian mixed up some kind of herbs and stuff into a paste and swabbed it on them and in a couple of days, he was as good as new. Said it stung a little, but that was all."

Hot said, "What kind of herbs and stuff?"

"Hell, I don't know. Didn't think to ask him. Didn't think it was important at the time. You want to try it?"

Hot conjured on this possibility for a while, then said, "Well, I don't see where it could be much worse without them being cut on, so I guess I'll try it. Let's go."

The "doctor" was in. His living room doubled as the office waiting room, and there Uncle Johnny sat and Hot stood after the initial examination, while the remedy was being prepared in the next room behind a closed door. After a few minutes of muted conversation between the policemen and muffled clattering in the next room, the door opened and the medico appeared holding a crock of mysterious substance from which protruded an eighteen inch stick of hickory. The end sticking down in the crock was wrapped with what looked like the remnants of an old dishtowel and tied on the stick with fishing line to make a swab.

Hot was instructed to again drop his britches and grab his ankles. This he did, peering up as best he could between his legs to make sure that the proper end of the stick was fixing to be used. Uncle Johnny took great interest in watching the procedure at as close range as he dared, which was standing right behind the squatting doctor with his chin an inch or two from the top of the doctor's shoulder. He had a pretty clear view. The doctor, pleased with the extreme thirst for knowledge which Uncle Johnny seemed to exhibit, took care to explain each step in the process, leaving Hot to his own thoughts and pursuits. He explained that this position would allow him to apply the mixture to all possible surfaces of the offending part unless he decided to pull gently on the extrusion to expose even more surface. At that statement, both Uncle Johnny and the doctor perceived a noticeable tightening in the field surrounding the point of interest, and the doctor hastened to add that in this particular case, he didn't think that procedure would be necessary. The field relaxed somewhat.

Hot had been pretty patient during the lecture, and undoubtedly was grateful that the doctor was explaining with such thoroughness the finer points of the procedures to Uncle Johnny. However, even his patience had a limit, and after about a full minute in the mooning position, suggested rather pointedly that he felt it best that they get on with it.

The doctor gave the mixture a final stir and gently began to daub the concoction on. Uncle Johnny glanced into Hot's upside down eyes and peripherally saw his jaw muscles knot up. Hot said, "Man, that stuff stings!" Then, "It's getting worse!" He let go of his ankles and placed his palms on the floor. His thighs started to quiver. "It ain't stinging anymore. It's *burning*! I mean, it's *burning*!....Gawd amighty!....Gawd *amighty*!....That's enough! I said, **THAT'S ENOUGH!!! AAAHHD DAMN!!!**"

Hot began to move away from his tormentor using his palms and shuffling his feet rapidly in baby steps, which was the best he could do with his britches still around his ankles.   When we was out of range of the swab, which had halted in mid air, he hollered at Uncle Johnny to "Git me to the house **NOW**!!!", snatched up his trousers as best he could and raced for the police car with Uncle Johnny, pistol and holster flapping, trying to catch up. The doctor, still holding the crock and swab, wisely decided that this was not the time to discuss the bill, and watched the cruiser leave a wiggly twin trail of smoking rubber even as the doors were still slamming shut.

They made it to Hot's house in what can only be called record shattering time. Before the car came to a stop, Hot was out and sprinting for the front door. Uncle Johnny decided that he'd done all he could do for him and drove the two blocks to his own house. He decided to call and check up on Hot's situation and Carrie answered the phone. Uncle Johnny asked if Hot had made it in O.K.

"Johnny, something is very wrong. The screen door was latched when he ran up on the porch, but I'm not worried about that. It can be fixed. I'm just thankful that we didn't have company here when he came in. His pants are lying in the hall, and his shorts are somewhere. He ran first to the bathroom, evidently looking to see if there was any water in the bathtub, which there wasn't, then to the kitchen sink, which was also dry. Then he jerked open the refrigerator. I had a big bowl of fresh cream I was planning to use over blackberry cobbler tonight sitting on the top shelf of the 'fridge. Hot snatched that bowl out, put it on the floor, and squatted over it. He's in there now muttering something about a 'sunofabitching Indian' and dipping both hands in the cream and sloshing it up...Johnny, you won't *believe* what he's doing with that cream! I can tell you that it won't be used on the blackberry cobbler. Johnny, are you O.K? You sound like you're choking. What in the world has happened?"

He was choking, of course. When he could finally talk, and could wipe the mirthful tears away, said, "Carrie, I really don't want to get into it. It's not serious. Hot will tell you later, I guess. Just in case he tries to leave while he's still talking about an Indian, please call me quick." Then, according to Uncle Johnny, he collapsed in a fit of howling glee until Aunt Alice got sort of interested and made him explain. Then she collapsed.

Now, the point of all this is that I'm not sure the phenomenon of sympathy mixed with mirth can be explained. I reckon my opinion is as good as any, and it's this:

Pain ain't funny. It's people that's funny.

GASTROINTESTINAL RUMBLINGS

I'm no cook. When I start cooking, even the flies leave the kitchen. My culinary capability consists of an average ability to smear mayonnaise on two pieces of bread and plop a slice of bologna (or is it baloney?) on one mayonnaise smeared side and gently place the other piece of bread on top. Occasionally when I pat the top bread slice in place, I discover that the mayonnaised side is face up. Then I carefully turn the top bread slice over and wash my hand.

I can make a pretty good bowl of popcorn if I have at my disposal the old pot part of a pressure cooker which I rescued for this purpose when my better half threw it away. I also foraged around and found a near-fitting pot lid to complete the ensemble, which now sits by the stove at all times. I've tried to wash the pot once or twice, but the grease drippings down the side of the pot from years of popping wouldn't wash, chip, or scour off, so I quit worrying about it. She just hides it now when company comes. I can also scramble an egg, and that usually works out O.K. if I put enough chopped-real-fine onion in it. Other than these three items, any food ingredient that I touch fire or boiling water to will generally turn into something that would give a buzzard colic.

I sometimes dream of preparing a sure enough big league candlelight dinner of fricasseed something-or-other replete with tender rice and vegetables and good wine all hot at the same time. Except the wine. Then when the folks ooh and aah about how good it is, I could sit back with just a hint of a smile and fend off compliments, like most cooks do.

My mother, who is one of the best cooks in at least the world, fends off compliments.

"Mama, these biscuits are *outstanding*!"

Does she say, "Thanks. And wasn't that squash casserole simply scrumptious?" She does not. She says, "I should have left those biscuits in the oven for just another minute. Then they would have browned prettier. Another pinch of salt wouldn't have hurt, either."

She knows very well that one more minute in the oven *would* have been too long, and that another pinch of salt *would* have hurt. Beats me.

When I was little, we had a maid named Esther Williams (not the swimming movie star). She was remarkably, extraordinarily, uncommonly wonderful. I loved her. Esther showed up every morning in her starched white uniform dress ready to handle any situation or chore in her unhurried, competent manner, whether it was housecleaning, playing cowboys and

Indians, paddling my rear if I needed it, or any of the dozens of other things she was called on to do. But where she really excelled was in the kitchen. And when she and my mother got together on the serious preparation of a meal, the stuff they put on the table was sinful. Anything that good had to be sinful.

She didn't use recipes. She just kind of felt her way along, and I don't remember a single failure. One time Mama asked Esther for her recipe on molasses cookies, which were the envy of the neighborhood. Esther said, "You takes a couple of double-handfuls of flour, two pinches of salt, etc., etc., and kneads it all together 'til it looks right. Then add three gullops of molasses and knead it again, then pinch off the cookies and put them in the oven 'til they're ready." Mama said, "Esther, I understand all of it but the gullops of molasses. What in the world is a *gullop*?"

"Aw, Miss Bobbie. You just throws the jug of molasses over your arm and pour. It says 'Gullop, Gullop, Gullop', and you cuts it off." *Man*, she could cook!

I've noticed something about cooking, though. Food prepared outside and eaten outside is generally passable if not downright delicious when the same stuff cooked and consumed inside would gag a maggot. I'm not talking about a backyard barbecue. That's usually done too close to the house. I'm talking about vittles created in the woods and wolfed down after a hard

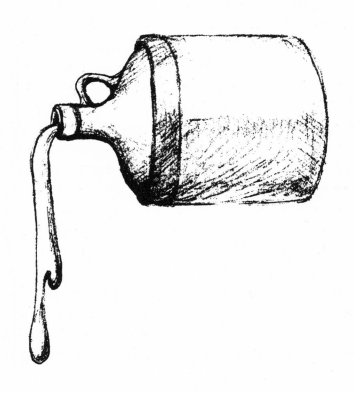

day's hunt. I've smelled dog food mixed with hot water in that setting that got my head close enough to the pan to where the dogs growled at me. I don't think I would have eaten any even if the dogs hadn't growled, but it sure smelled good.

The only times I didn't like outside food was when I was in the army. But somehow that shouldn't count. I was *told* to eat outside there, by God. And the cuisine wasn't anything to write home about. We had K-rations and C-rations most of the time in the field. If "A" stands for excellent and "F" stands for failure in the grading systems, they had those rations marked "K" graded about right. In the early 60's, I got a box of K-rations with a pack of Lucky Strike cigarettes in it that had a *green* wrapper. I understand that "Lucky Strike Green Goes to War!" was a familiar slogan once. But the war they were talking about was World War II, folks. Those rations I was eating had to be plus or minus twenty years old. I got to worrying about eating twenty-year-old meat. Not to worry, I was told. They preserved that stuff with something akin to embalming fluid, and that, I was told, would keep the meat from rotting for eons. After I gained that information, I traded meat for peaches and crackers. I don't know whether the embalming fluid bit was true, but nothing in an olive drab can tasted the same afterwards. I didn't reckon that peaches or crackers had to be embalmed.

I'd be less than honest if I didn't mention the only time I can remember (outside of the army) when a woods-cooked meal was absolutely inedible. My father cooked it. He wasn't used to cooking. We had my mother, you see, as I mentioned before.

On this particular occasion, my mother's brother, Uncle Johnny, my dad, my little brother, and I went on an all-night catfishing trip to the Bogue Chitto River around Brookhaven. We set out lines in the afternoon and ran them all night. To no avail. It was like the catfish had lockjaw that night. "But," my dad said, "just wait 'til I fix your breakfast! I'm gonna make you forget that we didn't catch any fish." He was right. He had brought some eggs, ham steak, and grits and planned to make "redeye" gravy out of the ham and river water. It was worse than awful. I still can't exactly figure what went wrong to make all of it taste sort of dirty metallic. My brother and I (we were 8 and 10 at the time) kind of picked around the edges, hoping against hope that the old "clean your plate" order wouldn't be voiced. Uncle Johnny saved us. He looked my dad straight in the eye and said, "Red, if Bobbie set something like this in front of you, there wouldn't be a judge in the world who wouldn't rule in your favor if you were to charge her with attempted murder." To his credit, and to our relief, my dad said, "You're right." And we loaded everything up and went to a cafe for breakfast.

I have on occasion found out, however, that just because something cooked at a camp is palatable, it isn't necessarily good for you. My bird dog and I were invited by Joe Hand to go on a Texas quail hunt one time down around San Antonio. (The dog was actually invited. They had to carry me because it was my

dog.) The first morning there, I started scrambling the eggs with the chopped-real-fine onions in them. The fellow who was hosting us took a keen interest in my preparation and found it was less than adequate. "Hell, boy, let me show you how we fix eggs in west Texas." Ground-up chili peppers, sloshed all over with Tabasco sauce, and God knows what else were stirred in the eggs. The resulting concoction was finally up to his standards after much tasting and addition of more chili peppers and Tabasco. After the first bite, and everything from the lips to the stomach was cauterized, they tasted pretty good. Those eggs stayed with me all day. And all through the next night. I was trying to sleep, and those eggs were doing battle with whatever they could find to do battle with. My stomach sounded like a championship dog fight. Even if the queasy feeling hadn't been considered, the noise would have kept me awake. The next morning, I could have bowed up and put those eggs through a keyhole at twenty feet. I mean the water in the toilet was absolutely whitecapping. And I discovered that the cauterizing effect didn't stop with the stomach. I made a mental note not to eat any more Texas-style eggs.

The best outside meal I ever ate will never be exactly duplicated. It won't be duplicated for the simple reason that nobody knows exactly what went into it. It was a pure community project with contributions from everyone who wished to participate. It didn't start out that way, but that's the way it turned out. And it was, as the saying goes, indescribably delicious.

We were at deer camp, and somebody decided that we should scour out the old wash pot that had been sitting in the middle of camp for years and which nobody could find a good use for, since things are not usually washed at deer camp. Clothes or people. Then, once the pot was relatively free of the mysterious residue which had accumulated on it, we could make a stew. Some of us thought that was a good idea (that night, after all the toasts to the deer, dogs, outdoor life, rifles, shotguns, Ducks Unlimited, and the Methodist Church, among other things, *anything* would have been a good idea), so we bustled around and hit the pot a few licks with some SOS pads to make it presentable. Maybe not presentable to the Pure Food and Drug Act folks, but it looked O.K. to us. Willie, the camp helper, did most of the work, since he had not participated too heavily in the toasting session.

We filled the pot about half full of water, built a fire around it, and when the water boiled, we began the scientific act of adding the ingredients. Some potatoes went in along with canned tomatoes, lots of salt and pepper, some of last year's celery salt that somebody's wife had brought to camp on a fishing trip the previous summer, and other things like that. We added a few pounds of deer meat, a squirrel or two, a duck or two, a couple of what was purported to be quail, and other things like *that*. Then we made sure that we had enough wood stacked around the pot to last the night, and went to bed.

The next morning, before we took up stands, we checked the stew, and it was doing fine. One of the pseudo cooks, who had been one of the main toasters the night before, and who had at least temporarily sworn off toasting, poured a fifth of Jack Daniels Black Label in "to give it a little twang." A couple of real dyed-in-the-wool hunters, who had passed on the toasting session, and who had killed a 'coon and a 'possum the night before, added these prizes to the stew that morning. Then we stacked enough wood around the pot to last the morning and went deer hunting.

We came in around noon to rest up and get ready for the afternoon hunt, and to check on the stew. It was still roiling and boiling and doing great. After a taste or two by a bunch of folks, we began to fine tune the taste. Some onions, hot sauce, a rabbit, meat tenderizer, and a few more twang ingredients were added. The stew had boiled down to where everything in it was pretty nondescript in a sort of mush. The bubbles that pushed up through all that stuff popped in a kind of a meaty "blup." A statement was made that somebody could fall in *that* stew and be forever unaccounted for. Then somebody hollered for Willie to fetch some more wood. No Willie. That was not like him not to be around when you needed him. The thought occurred to all of us at the same time that Willie was "unaccounted for." All eyes went to the stew.

"Blup....blup."

124

Nobody said anything, but we all dispersed in a hell of a hurry to look for Willie, and happily somebody found him asleep over by the skinning rack. A piece of wire mesh from the dog pen area was hurriedly put over the pot to satisfy any OSHA requirements, and we stacked enough wood around the pot to keep it going through the afternoon, and went back to the woods.

After we returned from the afternoon hunt, tired, cold, wet from a light all-afternoon drizzle, and hungry enough to eat the hind end out of a rag doll, we decided that the stew was ready, and we ate it. All of it. And if I had the exact recipe for that stew, my balance sheet would look better than IBM's. I have eaten in some multi-star restaurants all over the country, but I have never tasted anything that even remotely could measure up to that. I mean it was *outstanding*. And it gets better as the years go by.

My belly doctor told me shortly thereafter that I had an ulcer. But I'm not blaming the stew. Nothing that good could cause an ulcer.

HAPPY CAMPERS

Something strange happens to men at deer camp. Lots of familiar values change. Some would-be deer slayers come to camp in raggedy-assed old pickup trucks, some in monster-wheeled four-by-fours, and some in Jaguars or the equivalent, but once the vehicles are parked, it's hard to tell who's what. The wads of chewing tobacco cause just as much dribble on the chins of bankers as they do on the chins of fry cooks, and the engineer's understanding of logarithms has to give way to the woods wisdom of the grocery clerk. For the period of time you're at camp, class systems sort of evaporate because you can't spend money in the woods. (Unless the poker game is considered spending. Which it usually is for me.) The man who kills the biggest buck is the richest man there, followed by the one with the latest real war story escapade like having to climb a tree to get away from a bad-tempered wild hog on the south side of the big creek bend plum thicket. Then comes the one with the newest joke on one of the members present, then the loudest talker, then the biggest obvious liar.

The poorest man is a tie between the one who for some reason forgot to bring his whiskey and the one who is identified as the poor bastard who missed his shot at a buck standing broadside in the open. On second thought, one can generally beg a drink from somebody, but the miss can't be called back. And the buck who got missed is almost always the bull of the woods with a rack that's as big as a rocking chair. I saw a fellow miss one like that once, and the circumstances surrounding the missed shot made it an occasion worth remembering.

We had been at camp for a couple of days, and while there had been a lot of deer seen and shot at, we hadn't exactly set any records on the number we had hung on the skinning rack. At breakfast on the third day, I happened to be sitting next to a guest of one of the members. He was a pleasant, little, rotund, baldheaded fellow, and I can't remember his name. He should have been named Charles, though, because he looked like a "Chollie" (southern for Charley). Jolly Chollie. He was smiling and courteous and displayed the kind of deference anyone would who was at a place where he hadn't been before, and was kind of feeling his way around. He passed the biscuits and stuff real quick without having to be asked but once, and laughed at other folks' attempt at humor, and didn't say much except to answer direct questions. A real nice little fellow.

Our president of the club, name of Sonny, stood up as breakfast was ending and called for attention. Real loud.

"Boys, we've been missing too many deer. Jim and William and A.M. and I have been riding our asses off on those half-witted horses all day trying to keep up with the dogs and keep things stirred up so y'all can get a shot at a buck." He was talking about another Jim. Not me. This Jim was redheaded and his last name ended in an i. He told me one time that he was probably the only redheaded dago I'd ever meet.

"We've been doing *our* job," continued Sonny. "There's been more deer seen and shot at in the last couple of days than flies on a Mississippi State homecoming queen. Y'all just can't shoot, or you're not paying attention to what you're doing. So we're going to try something different. In the past, when anybody missed a shot, we've just cut off a piece of his shirttail and nailed it on the wall with a short note telling who, when, and so forth. Just like all the other clubs. But we've got so many shirttails on the walls now that the place looks like a quilt."

He glared at the assembly, which was unusually quiet. "From now on, anybody who misses a clear shot is going to get the hell beat out of him. The riders will see to that."

Now, Sonny, Jim, A.M., and William were all big men. I'm talking about *real* big men. And it was hard to determine which of them was more full of bullshit. This morning, though, that dubious honor seemed to belong to Sonny. The rest of us who knew him just nodded our agreement with his obviously well-thought-out ruling and said it was a good idea. No more missing. Or else. I happened to glance over at Chollie, and he was sort of half smiling. The other half of him wasn't so sure about how serious Sonny was. Sonny sure *seemed* serious. And he had just heard the true story about how the riders had caught a poacher on our club grounds one morning. They had handcuffed the violator around a cottonwood tree until the morning hunt was over. That meant that he was hugging that tree for about four hours. Then they delivered him to the sheriff and charged him with trespassing, giving him to understand that this was easy, compared to what he'd get if they caught him poaching again. Chollie seemed impressed with the firm, direct action which had been taken by the riders in this instance.

We drew numbers out of a hat to determine where our stands for the morning would be, and I drew a stand down on a logging road. Chollie drew a stand next to me on down the road a ways to my left. We were well out of shotgun range from each other, but I could see him pretty clearly.

Well, the dogs were turned loose right at first daylight and the hunt was on. The riders were hollering their encouragement to the dogs, and things were moving along like they should. The dogs jumped a deer within minutes of being turned loose and the woods echoed the music of a hound pack in full tongue. I noticed as the hunt wore on that the riders began to give full tongue too, and with the passage of time, they began to sound louder than the dogs. When one of the standers fired, the riders always rode to the sound of the shot to see if the hunter needed assistance with locating the deer he had hit. (Or missed, God help him.) But from the sounds that drifted through the woods, there wasn't much missing that morning. The riders got louder and louder with each shooting episode, and there seemed to be a short party held each time a hunter fired and the riders got to him.

Neither Chollie nor I had had the opportunity to take a shot, because all of the action seemed to be happening well north of our positions, which was to my right. All of a sudden, somebody south of us fired a shot, evidently spotting a deer slipping through the woods away from all the noise. The logging road where Chollie and I were stationed ran north and south, giving the best access for the riders to get from where they were to the most recent shot. Here they came, at a full gallop and hollering. They reined up briefly in front of me, and the phenomenon of the loud hollering cleared up. They weren't carrying guns and didn't have guns in their saddle holsters. But they did have bulging saddle bags, and the distinctive glassy clank emanating from those saddle bags coupled with the unsteady seat they all four had in their saddles solved the mystery. They had been toasting each deer killed. And they had obviously toasted several that morning. And they were undoubtedly enjoying the hell out of the hunt.

Now, we had strict rules at camp concerning drinking. Rifles and shotguns and whiskey don't mix. Anyone found drinking while carrying a loaded gun of any type was asked to leave camp and invited not to return. Period. No exceptions. Chollie had told me at breakfast that he liked that rule, since he didn't drink at all. But the riders weren't carrying guns. I reckon the drafters of the rules figured that if you wanted to risk breaking your own neck while riding, that was your business.

A.M., hanging on to the saddle horn with both hands, grinned broadly at me and informed me that the hunt was going good and that he had not had that much fun with his clothes on in a long time. Then in a shower of mud clods, they were off to check on the hunter south of us, waving to Chollie as they passed him. When they got to the hunter, I faintly heard another shout, "That's a beauty. A toast to the deer!!" Then, "Naw, that's an eight-point. We need to toast him *twice*!!" with garbled sounds of assent.

I was getting a little disappointed. There had been deer seen north and south of me and Chollie, and we hadn't seen a single one, and it was getting on up to about ten o'clock. We'd been on the stands since before daybreak, and in about another thirty minutes or so, the jeep would be by to pick us up. So I was straining at each little sound or movement to try and conjure up a buck by sheer will power. It wasn't working.

I glanced to my left and saw Chollie ease to my side of a tree, looking to *his* left. From the scrub, a monster buck stepped out into the road and stopped broadside to me and Chollie, looking south to where all the latest toasting sounds were coming from. He looked to me to be out of shotgun range from Chollie, but at that distance, I couldn't be sure. Chollie seemed to be rassling with that same thought. He had his gun raised, and was probably praying that the buck would come on up the road toward us. The deer stood motionless for a full two minutes. He was a long way from me, but even at that distance I could tell that he was really something special. The sun glinted off those massive horns, and Chollie was having to watch and pray and hope.

The buck, still watching south, took a step or two toward the other side of the road, obviously intending just to cross and not come up our way, and stopped again, still broadside to us, and in the wide open. I could tell what Chollie was thinking. If he didn't shoot, the deer was gone, so the only choice he had was to aim high and hope for a miracle. He decided to take the chance, and his shotgun boomed. The deer, unscratched for sure because his tail was straight up, took off for other parts while the sound of Chollie's shot reverberated through the woods. The dejected Chollie slumped down beside his tree, and I decided to walk on down to him, figuring he might be in need of some consoling. He didn't wait for me to speak and said, "I just missed the biggest buck in the woods." I told him that I'd seen the whole thing. "I had to try it,"" he said, sort of apologetically. "I've never even seen a buck like that, let alone had a shot at one. So I just had to try." I lied and told him I'd have done the same thing.

Well, the deer and I weren't the only ones who'd heard the shot. Chollie's head snapped around when we heard the riders whoop and start our way.

"Aw, *shit*."

I didn't reply. A thin film of sweat began to appear on his upper lip.

Here they came again, mud flying and hooves thundering. I understood at that moment how foot soldiers must have felt in the face of a cavalry charge. They looked intimidating. Big men on big horses, bridle bits jangling, horses and men snorting, and steam rising from all of them. Looked like a small mountain range riding up.

"Whur's the deer?"

Nobody said anything. I was looking down and shuffling a little, halfheartedly kicking at a leaf.

"We thought we heard a shot from around here." No reply. Sonny looked at me as best he could, afflicted as he was, and said, "Jim, didn't you just shoot?"

"Naw."

"Well, *somebody* did." I stayed quiet.

"I did," Chollie finally gulped.

"Well, whur's the deer?"

Chollie breathed almost inaudibly, "I missed him."

"What?"

"I missed him."

Sonny's countenance turned dark. "You *missed* him!?" Chollie hesitated a second and then nodded.

Sonny slowly swung his right leg over his horse's rump and stepped down, sort of Clint Eastwood style. I stole a glance at

Chollie, and his color didn't look too good. Kind of grayish green. A big bead of sweat defied the cold morning and rolled out from under his cap and down his jaw.

Sonny turned, fumbled in his saddle bag and faced Chollie with a brand new fifth of bourbon and a smile as wide as a piano keyboard. He handed the bottle straight out to Chollie and said, "Well, hell. Let's toast the *miss!*"

The look that came over Chollie would have made a revival preacher certain that the man's whole life had changed before his very eyes. Ol' non-drinker Chollie reached out and grabbed that jug by its neck and turned it straight up. Big bubbles fairly bounced off the bottom of the bottle as his adam's apple bobbed in concert. After about three fingers' worth had disappeared, he handed the bottle back to Sonny, and the miss was duly toasted by all others present. But maybe with a little less enthusiasm than Chollie had shown. Then the riders took off in high gear to stir things up again in the north.

I suggested to Chollie that we unload the guns and enjoy the sounds of the hunt while we waited for the jeep. And we did. Chollie, his gaze following the path of the riders' departure, half grinned at me and said, "They're good old boys, ain't they?"

I said yeah.

A SORT OF CONFESSION

Murder is a dark and ugly word. It sounds even more repugnant when you may be guilty of it, which I may be. I don't know whether it was actually murder or not. Sometimes I think it was, and sometimes I don't. You can be the judge of that. I was never prosecuted by the law for it. I'm sometimes prosecuted by my conscience.

I killed a friend of mine. With a rifle, and with what the law calls "malice aforethought," even though the period of "afore-thought" was only about five minutes. It was not done in a period of anger, nor in a period of "temporary insanity," nor was it accidental, nor was it because of righteous jealousy, nor done in self-defense. I simply pointed a rifle between his eyes and pulled the trigger. And he died instantly. His name was Tom. His registered, legal name was Frierson's Tom Boy. He was an orange and white English Pointer. He wasn't the very best bird dog I ever owned, but in the important things, he was the most special. He was hardheaded, bad to fight, almost unpennable, and a semi-outlaw. And he loved me. And I loved him. I still do.

I first met Sir Tom on the heels of another tragedy. I had just lost the best bird dog I'd ever hunted behind. I mean he was *perfect*. I had trained him myself from his puppyhood. He could find quail like he used radar, he was staunch on point, he honored other dogs on point as far as he could see them, he was like a vacuum cleaner finding dead birds, and he retrieved to hand without mussing a feather. His name was Rip, and he was a gentleman. I almost never had to even raise my voice to him. I simply turned him loose and let him perform.

When I lost Rip, I immediately started looking for another dog. I decided this time to buy a trained dog and settled temporarily on probably the most beautiful pointer I'd ever seen. His name was Beau, and he absolutely drew stares wherever we went. He was gorgeous. A classic lemon and white pointer whose style on point would make the hair on the back of your neck stand up. Problem was that the sound of a shot would cause him to flinch. He wouldn't flinch bad, but he would flinch enough for me to suspect that he was a little soft.

Pete Frierson told me when I bought him to bring him back if I had any problem with him. So I took him back to Pete and explained the problem. I told him that I would really prefer to have a dog who was a little bolder. Pete said, "Son, if bold is what you're after, I think you'll like this one." That's when I met Sir Thomas.

Pete's trainer, Fred Bridges, walked me over to Tom's pen and introduced us. "Jim," Fred drawled, "you know I'll shoot straight with you. This is a good dog. He's got a good nose and he knows what to do. But in my forty years of training dogs, I can honestly say that this is the hard-headedest, cantankerdest, orneriest dog I have ever handled. He can climb out of Alcatraz, he'll fight another dog in a New York minute, and he'll try your patience in every way a dog can try a man until you convince him that you're his boss. You're going to have to put your bull in his pasture and not let him get away with the least little thing until you convince him that you're serious about what you tell him to do. But once you remove his doubts, I think you'll be pleased with him. If you aren't, bring him back and we'll keep trying 'til we find one that suits you."

I looked at the three year old dog, and he looked at me. I got the distinct feeling that we were actually appraising each other. He was about average size for a pointer, but he was wide-chested and had a pretty heavy coat of muscle. I figured he weighed about sixty pounds. His head was wide, leaving plenty of room for brains between those amber eyes which met my gaze in a straightforward look that left no doubt in my mind that he was alert, bright, and confident. His tail was up and wagging in short, muscular whips. His muzzle was a little too short for him to be a really good looking dog, and his big mouth was open with a long tongue hanging out one corner in a kind of lopsided, tongue-lolling grin. I didn't even look at another dog. As he loaded into my car, Fred, after telling me the commands he used with Tom, reminded me, a little differently this time, "Remember, Jim, if you don't like him, or *can't handle him*, bring him back."

I never took him back, but I did consider it a few times in the beginning. I found out on our first hunting trip that Fred had described Tom to a "T." The frustrating part of dealing with him was that he *knew* what I wanted him to do, but was enough of a delinquent to just challenge me either by not paying a bit of attention to my commands, or worse, pausing to let me know that he heard and understood, then proceeding to do whatever the hell he wanted to do. Which was almost never what I wanted him to do.

Now, I don't like corporal punishment. I didn't like to get it, and I never liked to give it. To my kids or to my dogs. And I always used it as the absolute last resort. But with Tom, I figured there was no other way, and the trainer's advice seemed more and more to acquire validity. Except in Tom's case, corporal punishment wasn't enough. After a good switching with a whippy hickory, he'd grin as if to say "Thanks, Boss," and go his merry way again. Corporal punishment escalated to sergeant punishment, then to captain, then to colonel. The first three times I took him out, I shot him a total of five times.

I'd command "Come here," he'd pause, look at me, and head in the other direction. When I was sure that the eyes and vital parts weren't exposed, and when enough distance was between us, I'd burn his fanny with number 8s and he would turn and come to me. Finally, after the fifth shot on the third trip, I guess he decided that when I said "Come here," I meant *Come Here*, and we never had that problem again. Once we settled that little misunderstanding and I was able to call him to me, I had to add another item of equipment to my arsenal. It was a piece of rubber hose about two feel long. I'm talking about the reinforced kind that you hook up washing machines with. The regular rubber hoses didn't last long with Tom.

Now, before you get all stirred up about what a cruel S.O.B. I am who would shoot a poor dog with birdshot and tear his rear up with a rubber hose, and before you pick up that phone to call the Society for the Prevention of Cruelty to Animals, you need to understand that I was dealing with a special case here. Tom was... well, he was...*physical*. That's what he was. Physical. He'd point, then run the birds up, come to me when I called him, cheerfully take his whipping, and head out again. I think he was sort of Presbyterian because he always seemed glad to get that predestined event over and go on to the next situation. He never pouted or became cowed, even when I really got tough with him.

One time Bill Cook and I were hunting with Tom and my other dog, Sue, and it had been a long, unproductive day. The quail had just seemed to evaporate from the face of the earth. We hadn't located a single one all day. Finally, in the afternoon, old Susie pointed right up on the top of a bald hill in short grass. Tom rounded the crest of the hill, saw her pointed, and skidded to a perfect honoring point like a gentleman should, about ten yards behind her. Bill and I kicked into high gear to get up there and flush the birds. It was going to be an ideal situation where a wide open shot was inevitable and we were both thinking of a double or a triple each. At last, some excitement!

Tom sort of got excited too, I guess. Just before we got into gun range, for reasons known only to him, he shot past Susie and ran those birds up. Must have been about thirty of them fanning out in a storybook covey rise. Then the culprit decided to chase a low flying bird which, fortunately, led him right by me. I tackled him, grabbed his collar, took a half turn in the collar so he couldn't pull out, put a foot on his hindquarters, and went to work on him with the hose, hollering "Whoa" with every lick.

Well, I whipped him until I thought I was going to have a heart attack. When I finally quit, he didn't get up. I hadn't realized that when I took the turn on his collar, I had cut off his wind. He was sort of unconscious. I reached down and pumped on his ribs a few times and he got up and staggered around for a minute. Then he looked at me as if to say, "O.K., I think I understand. Now, which way did those birds go?" In less than five minutes he was frozen on a single point, and he honored Susie's point several times later that afternoon. That day was the last time he failed to honor a point. I even found him pointed in the woods once honoring an old refrigerator somebody had dumped. I guess he figured the white thing might be another dog, and he wasn't close enough to see that it wasn't. And maybe he was remembering....

All of the situations weren't exasperating. After a while, the trips began to take on more of a bird hunting flavor instead of arm-thrashing exercise sessions, and the diminishing number of violations sometimes even added a little humor.

He was stuck on a single bird one afternoon, pointing solid as a rock. He had the bird dead to rights and I was on my way to him when I saw the danger signal flash. His tail, normally rigid at about a sixty degree angle, was moving slightly side-to-side. This meant one of three things: A. He wasn't sure he had the bird located; B. He wasn't sure what it was he was pointing; or C. More likely than A or B, he was going to flush the bird himself. This particular time, he performed C. The quail went whirring off, I called him to me, and he and I and the rubber hose had our regular meeting. After the meeting, he disappeared over the hill in front of us which was, in fact, just where I wanted him to go. When I reached the top of the hill, there was Tom, rock-solid pointed again in a patch of broomsage. And his tail started moving again. I admit to having had a sinking feeling because I was worn out from our last little tete-a-tete, and I wasn't sure I could perform effectively again that quickly. So I hollered "Whoa," just to let him know I was watching. I knew that his fanny had to still be burning. At the sound of my voice, four deer jumped up from their beds in the broomsage ahead of Tom and took off lickety-split. Tom didn't move. Then he slowly turned his head and looked at me and said without speaking, "Look, *you* ran them up. I didn't even know what they were. But I figured I'd better wait 'til you got here. So leave that hose in your hunting sack." I grinned and sent him on.

Lord, how he loved to fight! He was a perfect gentleman as long as he was around a female dog, but with the slightest provocation from another male, Tom would be on him like white on rice and he'd hang with it 'til times got better. Or until I'd somehow break it up.

I've always kept my bird dogs penned. (In Tom's case, the pen floor was concrete and the pen had to have a completely wired top.) The neighborhood we lived in at this particular time was occupied by a big German Shepherd who ran loose and was the scourge of the other canine neighborhood occupants. He was a bully who had whipped every unpenned dog in the area. There was no question as to who was king of that hill.

One afternoon I turned Tom and Sue loose for an exercise run in a large field nearby and I was following a leisurely couple of hundred yards behind them, just keeping them in sight. I saw that big shepherd come sailing out of some high grass and make a snapping pass at Susie. Tom was on him in a heartbeat. By the time I ran to them, blood was flying in all directions and a sure enough serious dogfight was in progress. I sort of dived in the middle of it and somehow got them apart, swooped up the bloody Tom in my arms, and ran home to survey the damage. I gingerly began to wash off the blood, dreading what I might find. The more I washed, the more puzzled I became. None of the blood was his. There wasn't a nick on him. I couldn't believe he had given away twenty pounds to a heavyweight German Shepherd and had come out unquestionably on top. But he had. He turned his head and looked at me with that lopsided, tongue-lolling grin and I'll swear he was trying to tell me, "That was fun! I enjoyed the fight and the bath, but Boss, I especially enjoyed the ride home!" And the shepherd gave our house a wide berth after that day.

Like I said earlier, Tom was physical. He liked for me to put my hands on him or to just *touch* him in some way. When I'd turn him out of his pen, he'd dance around me and grin and bounce like most dogs do, but he wouldn't jump up on me because he knew I didn't allow that. Still he had to touch somehow, so he'd dance around behind me and *nibble* at the seat of my pants. No bites, or even nips. More like bounce and nibble and bounce and nibble. Anything for friendly contact.

His downfall started one day when he and I were hunting alone on our farm. He had pointed a covey of birds and was standing in a patch of knee high honeysuckle. He wasn't broken to wing and shot, so when I kicked the birds up, he jumped as he always did. I didn't see exactly what happened, but one of the honeysuckle vines evidently tripped him up. In any event, he landed some freak way so that he shattered his right shoulder. I heard one little yelp of pain. No loud screaming or crying, though the pain must have been fierce. Just that one little yelp. My truck was parked at the house three-quarters of a mile away. I bedded him down in the honeysuckle and raced to the truck so I could pick him up and rush him to the vet. I bumped over that pasture in the pickup like there was no tomorrow and when I got to where I'd left him, he wasn't there. A frantic search followed and I finally found him about halfway home. He had an absolutely shattered shoulder and had tried to quietly follow me home.

After the trip to the vet's office, the x-rays, the cast, the pills, etc., I took him home, but irreparable damage had been done. For several weeks he'd try to walk, but the cast was too long and bulky to allow it, so the best he could do was a sort of dragging shuffle, and he began to weaken. After a couple of subsequent trips to the vet, I was advised that I should leave him there to be put down.

I had to think about that for a while, so I took him home that final time. He was nine years old, and the old recuperating ability just wasn't there. I resigned myself after two days of thinking about it that the vet's suggestion would be the best course, so the next morning I went to his pen to get him and carry him on his last journey.

He was lying on his belly too weak to move anything but his head and tail. I picked him up and carried him out of the pen to a shady spot where we could talk. And I talked, and he listened for a change. It was then that I decided on a slightly different course. We had walked too many miles together, shared too many triumphs together, and loved each other too much for me to allow him to die under the hands of a relative stranger in the one confusing, antiseptic place he hated. So I got up, went into the house and got my rifle, loaded it, and killed him.

148

I wrapped him in a good bedsheet from the house, placed him in the pickup along with a shovel, and started our one vehicle procession to the north forty for the burial. I picked out a grave-site in a grove of oaks where he had found his last covey of birds before the accident, and started to dig.

I don't cry much. Real men don't do that, I'm given to understand. But that day I exited the ranks of real men for the first time in twenty years. I'd forgotten that the first tears burn as badly as sweat in the eyes and that a contraction begins deep down in the groin and that involuntary spasmodic jerks move up the abdomen to the gut and the chest and strangled noises perco-late up through all that to a tight throat and blast out loud enough to be heard for a quarter of a mile. I'd forgotten that mucus and saliva mix into strings tough enough so that when you try to spit, the strings won't turn loose and have to be semi-smeared on a shoulder or a sleeve. I'd forgotten that during the course of all this carrying on, it helps to be able to *attack* some-thing like tough goddam oak roots with a goddam dull shovel in hard, dry goddam dirt so that the main attention can be turned to the difficult physical task at hand and slow the goddam crying. That works for a few minutes until the corner of the eye acciden-tally catches a glimpse of a bloody sheet, and the whole goddam process starts all over again.

The burial took hours. Then, when I'd dried out inside and outside, I drove back to the house and smilingly told the family that I'd buried old Tom in a good place.

That occurred years ago. Time, of course, has dimmed the event some, but I still remember one small segment as if it had happened this morning. Just before I pulled the trigger, he looked me straight in the eye, grinned that lopsided grin, and scraped his tail across the ground in a feeble wag. I think he was trying to tell me he understood. I hope I was right. I hope he understood.

Please, God, I hope he understood.

SOUTHERN STYLE

S outherners are a different breed of cat. It's hard to explain
to other folks how we operate. Especially in the humor
department. You don't have to have a real knee-slapping,
loud, raucous, hollering laughter situation to create a truly
mirthful condition. And a lie ain't all bad if the conditions are
right, and you don't just tell one outright. It's, like I said, hard to
explain. I'll just try and give you an example.

A few years ago in Natchez, a yankee, down for the world-
famous Natchez Pilgrimage, was having lunch at a local restaurant
and was complaining to his bride about the high cost of frog legs
on the menu. He was overheard by one of the local sportsmen,
name of Bubba. Bubba, being the self-appointed ambassador of
good will for the community that the Chamber of Commerce
seemed to approve of, loudly agreed with the man and offered to
take him frog gigging to give him a new hunting experience and to
get him some inexpensive frog legs. The visitor, against the advice
of his bride, accepted the invitation, obviously looking for a

diversion from the hoop skirts and antique furniture and mansions and lectures on "the way it was" stuff he'd been subjected to for days.

That night they loaded up Bubba's old aluminum boat in the back of his pickup and headed for a local lake. They launched the boat and Bubba, sitting up front and holding the light, paddled the boat, holding the three-tined gig ready with the leather thong in the handle of the gig wrapped around his wrist. He spotted a bullfrog sitting on a lily pad and pointed him out to the yankee, who was sitting on the back seat. Then he eased up to the frog and jabbed hard. The frog jumped away just in time and the gig stabbed through the lily pad and into the thick, back hide of a ten-foot alligator who had been lurking unseen under the pads with designs on the frog himself.

Well, the 'gator roared and went to splashing and rocking the boat, as you can imagine. Bubba dropped the light to the bottom of the boat before the yankee could see what was happening and started trying to snatch the gig out of the 'gator's tough hide. It was pitch black dark, so all the yankee could do was grab both sides of the boat, hang on, hope Bubba knew what he was doing, and listen to that frog roar. (Leastwise he *thought* it was the frog.)

Bubba had his own problems, since the leather thong was around his wrist and he couldn't let go. But after a couple of lunges and somersaults by the 'gator, the gig came loose. The 'gator skedaddled, leaving a couple of serious dents and about three inches of water in the boat, along with one pale, shook up yankee, who hadn't seen anything in the dark, but had been bounced around and splashed pretty good. Bubba picked up the light and shined it on the gig, which had one tine pointing east, another west, and the third straight up, and then he shined the light on the yankee.

Now, Bubba is not what you would call a real liar, but when he saw the state the yankee was in, he was opportunist enough to realize that he had a situation possibility that he could share in the future around the truck stop cafe with some of his cronies. He calmly informed the yankee that he was glad the frog got off.

"The game wardens are awful tough on size limits this year," said Bubba, "and I saw right away that little frog was not big enough to legally keep. We'll ease around to the other side of the lake and see if we can find some really big ones."

The yankee informed Bubba that he had a severe sinus condition that was beginning to become a problem because of the heavy humidity on the lake and a bad back and that he was allergic to mosquitoes and a few other ailments that he conjured up in a hurry, and that Bubba had best paddle him over to where the truck was parked and let him sit in the truck for a while until all of this stuff settled down. He didn't want to ruin the frog gigging expedition, so Bubba could just go on hunting frogs while he recuperated. In the truck.

Bubba dutifully paddled him to the bank by the truck, sympathizing with each of the symptoms which had been

155

described to him, voicing his appreciation that the yankee was courteous enough to suffer in the truck by himself and not cut the hunt short, let the yankee out of the boat, eased on out into the dark, and headed for the other side of the lake.

When he got to the other side, he'd locate a frog, shine the light just long enough to gig him, cut the light off, and bang the side of the boat with the paddle, splash around, yell a bunch, and in general create enough disturbance so that the yankee would understand that the battle had been joined.

After about an hour of this, Bubba returned with his catch wriggling inside a croaker sack, and looking much the worse for wear. The yankee, who seemed to have regained his health, reached for the sack to help the bedraggled Bubba unload the boat. Bubba said, "I'd be a little careful with that sack. The last frog I gigged had just grabbed a pretty fair sized cottonmouth moccasin by the nape of his neck, and I couldn't make the son of a bitch turn him loose. So I just sacked the both of them. He's probably lost interest by now and has spit him out, and the snake is likely wandering around somewhere in the sack, and with all that wiggling, it's hard to figure which is him and which is frogs."

The yankee snatched back his hand and let Bubba, worn out as he was, beach and land the boat, stow the gig and paddle, and especially handle the sack. On the way back to town, in the course of their conversation, the yankee reckoned as how he hadn't figured in the effort that went into harvesting frog legs and that the price didn't seem so high after all.

Now you can see that Bubba didn't just come out and tell a bald-faced lie. Except about the snake, but that was sort of incidental and minor, and was probably done without a lot of forethought. The whole operation was just kind of drifted along with and natural conditions dictated what the action would be, and...well, if you don't understand what I'm saying, because I'm kind of balled up in trying to find the right words to tell you, just ask any Southerner what I mean. Especially if he hunts or fishes. I really believe he will do his best to explain. And I can almost guarantee that he won't lie to you. Outright.

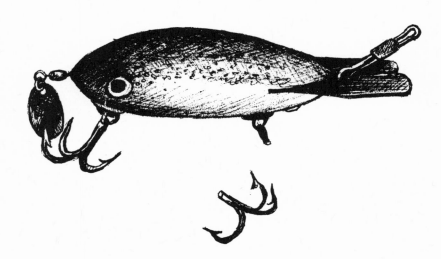

THE MAKING OF A WEEDLESS DIVE BOMBER

I've caught a lot of bass using a plug called the Dive Bomber. It's a funny looking lure, with a sort of paddle on the front end which causes it to go deeper the faster you retrieve it, and it has two treble hooks on it, and I customized mine by putting a little spinner thing on the back end. When you retrieve it, the paddle end goes down and the tail end goes up and the whole thing wiggles and vibrates and the spinner spins and bass just love it enough to try and devour it. Or hate it enough to try and kill it. I don't know which emotion causes it, but it catches fish anyway. Problem is, when you fish it, sometimes the front set of hooks snag on the bottom, so some fishermen simply take a pair of heavy wire cutters and snip off the front hooks, thereby making what they call a "weedless" Dive Bomber. (It ain't really weedless. But with only one set of treble hooks, it only catches half as many weeds as it would with two. If it was really weedless, that would mean no hooks. And it would also mean that you could cast it forever and not catch a bass. Which might seem pointless to you, but if you think about it, you could spend a lot of money on tackle and licenses, make your bass plugs truly weedless, and be in the running for Conservationist of the Year.)

I made a weedless Dive Bomber once, but it took the help of a friend of mine. And it took several hours. And it involved a considerable amount of beer and a hospital emergency room and...well, it all started off in a pretty routine manner, as most war stories do.

Bill Jackson used to be my across-the-street neighbor before I up and moved to Shocco. We lived in a normal, quiet, pretty suburb, where most folks piddled around in the yard and flower beds on Saturdays, went to church on Sundays, went to work on the weekdays, and sometimes cooked a steak in the back yard.

Bill was a little different. His job didn't have regular hours. He was a paper products sales manager for a large company, and one of the main things he sold was paper diapers. The rest of us in the neighborhood sold stuff like computers or food products or insurance or sporting goods and other real important things. Bill sold paper diapers. And he got home early a lot. Many afternoons I'd come home and a bunch of the young wives in the neighbor- hood (including mine) would be standing around in his driveway chatting with Bill and his wife Ellen (who was cute as a button, by the way).

Since he was the only male in the bunch, he was usually the center of attention, and all of the girls knew him. Now, I don't mean to imply anything about this except...well, he did get home early a lot and he knew all of the girls and he sold paper diapers and...I don't know how I got off on that. I just happened to remember that his next door neighbor, Ron, mentioned it to me one time and...well, that has nothing to do with the weedless Bomber. Get thee behind me, Satan.

Bill decided one day to buy himself a boat. It was a sixteen foot runabout, powerful enough to pull two skiers, and he also viewed it as a fishing boat. He knew I liked to fish and suggested to me on several occasions that we go out to the reservoir and try our hand at catching some bass. In his new boat. I kept telling him that I thought the boat's motor hung too low to allow us to fish in the shallow water where I usually had the best luck. But Bill was originally from Missouri. And he had seen some of those boys on TV talking about fishing on "structure" and on deep drop-offs and all that stuff and based on that, he figured big bass stayed in deep water and hang the water temperature and time of year and all that stuff and he wanted to catch a bass big enough to hang on the wall and this was Saturday and Ellen and Perry were taking the kids to the movie this afternoon and he had a case of beer iced down and the boat was waiting and the reservoir was waiting and how about it?

I finally said O.K.

I said O.K. with some reluctance, because I'd seen his tackle box. Those of you who fish a lot will understand what my concern was. There was no rust. No gunk. No spilled oil in it. No rubber skirts stuck to plastic worms so that when you try to separate them, they protested by extruding a long string of rubber-plastic, colored like skirt and worm mixed, which sticks to your fingers and stinks. Most of his plugs were still in their boxes. The rest were still shrink-wrapped. And the killing telltale sign: his fish stringer was unused with the rubber band still around it. It didn't take a rocket scientist to realize that I had a neophyte on my hands. With a new ski boat with a low-hanging motor, with ski ropes everywhere, with a paint job with those little sparkly things in it, with a console but no live well in it, with a stereo but no electric trolling motor, and with built-in ash trays and swinging beverage holders but no electric anchor motors. But he did have a case of beer iced down, and I said to myself, "What the hell." It was too hot to cut the grass, and the flower beds were Perry's idea in the first place and she and Ellen were taking the kids to an air conditioned movie. And Bill did have a case of beer iced down. And he was good company, and I hadn't ridden really fast in a boat in a while, and there was always the possibility that we might get into a school of bass hanging over a drop-off, and I hadn't tried out my new reel, and he really did have a case of cold beer iced down.

So we loaded all our gear in the sparkly boat, hooked it behind his car, and roared off to the reservoir to pursue the wary black bass. Who evidently were in shallow water, like I thought they were. And since his low hanging motor wouldn't allow us to get in shallow water, they were left in peace to glide and cavort and attack surface lures and spinner baits offered by real fishermen whose boats couldn't pull skiers. And whose boats weren't painted with all that sparkly stuff.

We fished in unpopulated deep water until most of the beer was gone and the sun was mercifully dipping into the horizon, and the singing of mosquitoes suggested that we'd best crank that powerful, low-hanging, skiing motor and head back to the suburb. We'd been skunked. Not one strike had been had by either one of us, let alone hooking the wall-hanger bass that Bill still insisted was lurking under us. I tried to tell him that if a bass was lurking around the bottom of the lake right under us, he would probably look like a knife blade, since pressure at that depth would crush a nuclear submarine. But he was unconvinced.

"I *know* he's there," he said. "Don't you have a lure in your tackle box that you haven't tried yet? I read in a magazine about this fellow who was on the verge of getting skunked and who discovered that he had overlooked one plug and put it on and caught a whole stringer full in no time."

I told him I enjoyed fiction, too. But, to mollify him, I rummaged around in the disaster area of my tackle box and, behold! Up popped my trusty Dive Bomber! I couldn't believe I'd not even had it wet all afternoon. Maybe it was a sign from somewhere that he'd read that story, and one of my favorite plugs hadn't even been tried yet! Out of the mouths of babes...who drink beer and sell paper diapers.

I hurriedly tied on my Dive Bomber and reared back to cast it as far as I possibly could so that I'd have enough distance to retrieve it fast and let it wiggle and spin down to where old bucket-mouth might be waiting. With a mighty heave, I whipped the rod up and out and ZZZZZZZTT! You fishermen have heard that sound. My reel had backlashed into several Gordian Knots. Right behind that, another strange sound. Sort of a high pitched, garbled, half scream that when translated said, "Wait a goddam minute!" and, "Don't move anything!" and several other things that I don't feel comfortable about telling you.

Well, to be honest, I used a few semi-colorful words myself, since I'd never seen a backlash as utterly hopeless as the bird's nest of line I was looking at in my new reel. I looked around to tell Bill about the backlash, and the reason for the mishap was immediately apparent.

There he sat, looking at me with doleful eyes and with my Dive Bomber sitting right on top of his fat head. I'm talking about right up on the place where if you put your finger between your eyes and run it in a straight line back over the top of your skull, when your finger starts downward, that locates the spot where my Dive Bomber was. Right up on that little pointed bump. (I'm assuming your head is pointed like mine is.) One of the front treble hooks had found a home right in that spot. The rest of the Dive Bomber was hanging down the back of his head like a jingling, rattling, pigtail.

"Bill, you ain't going to believe what you've done to my reel," I said, trying to keep my temper under control. I honestly had never seen a backlash that bad before.

What Bill told me to do with my backlashed reel is biologically impossible without extreme physical discomfort.

I was surprised at his sudden shift away from his sunny disposition. I got a glimpse into his dark side. He sat very still, glowering at me, and suggested in a firm voice that I put my rod down and separate him from my Dive Bomber. Now.

So I put down my rod and backlashed reel and made my way back to him for a damage inspection. He was damaged. The hook was buried up to the curved part in his fat scalp where the thin hair was. Way past the barb. I wiggled it a little, and more expletives poured forth from him than I thought was necessary.

I said, "Bill, try not to be so emotional about this, and hand me those pliers in my tackle box." That settled him down a little. He wilted slightly and said, "Maybe we ought to think about this for a minute. What are you planning to do with those old rusty pliers?"

"I'm going to snatch that hook out."

"Hold it. I ain't too crazy about that idea," he said. "Just cut the hook off the plug for right now and let's let somebody who knows what the hell he's doing get the hook out."

Well, I'm more thick-skinned than most, but that remark stung. I bowed up a little and said, "Now, look. I got several problems with that plan. First of all, these pliers won't cut through that thick hook. Second, I can snatch the thing out as good as anybody. And third, I ain't about to cut any hooks off my only Dive Bomber." The very idea. His priorities were obviously way out of whack.

"Keep those pliers away from my head and let's get to an emergency room," he said, with a voice which sounded more cordial. "I'll wear this thing 'til then."

I really didn't think a trip to the emergency room was necessary, since I could have had the hook out in no time, leaving only a gash of a half inch or so, and not too deep, since the space between his scalp and skull wasn't very thick even considering it was pretty fat. But he wasn't being very cooperative, so I quit suggesting it. I did, however, suggest that we take the boat back home so we wouldn't have to fight the Saturday evening traffic around the hospital while towing the boat.

He agreed, and cranked the powerful skiing motor and roared to the loading ramp with enough speed that my Dive Bomber streamed straight out behind his fat head with the little spinner thing spinning so fast I was worried that he'd break it. But I didn't say anything about it. I just thought it was a little inconsiderate of him.

We loaded the sparkly boat onto his trailer and headed for home, with Bill driving and nodding his head forward so that the empty hooks on my Dive Bomber wouldn't latch onto the velour of his car seat's head rest and create another problem. The drive home went without further incident, if you don't count the

jeepload of teenagers we pulled up next to at a traffic light. They
seemed interested in the Dive Bomber Bill was wearing, and some
animated conversation and finger-pointing ensued. Bill looked
kind of sheepish and turned his face toward me so they wouldn't
identify him, which gave them a pretty good view of the Dive
Bomber. The light finally turned green and they blasted off,
probably in search of the store which sold this latest fashion in
creative head ornamentation.

When we got home, we unhooked the trailer and discovered
that Perry and Ellen had not yet returned from their excursion
with the kids. Since I've been well trained, I hurriedly left a note
for Perry so she wouldn't worry. It said, "We've gone to the
emergency room. Be back later." Seemed O.K. to me. She asked
me later not to leave any more notes like that without a little more
detailed information. Asked it pretty emphatically. Some days it
seems you just can't win, no matter how thoughtful you try to be.

I drove Bill to the emergency room of the big local university
hospital. I let him out of the car at the entrance, parked the car in
the parking lot, and sauntered back to wait with him. There was a
uniformed attendant in front of the door, whose function
evidently was to handle special emergencies or belligerents. He
was big enough to do either. He caught me by the elbow as I
started in and asked, "Aren't you the one who brought in that guy
with the fish hook in his head?" I said yeah.

"Who hooked him... you or him?"

"I did."

He grinned and said, "You gonna have him mounted?"

Well, that was the first smile I'd seen in a while, and I was grateful for that. I said, "Nope. He's big enough to mount, I reckon, but his shape and color ain't perfect. He'd look awful." That seemed to please the attendant, who grinned a little broader and shook his head and reassumed his post.

I walked into the emergency room waiting area, which was inhabited by a crowd of folks with the usual complaints you'd expect to find in a Saturday evening emergency room. Cuts and bruises stemming from various personal disagreements, bumps and abrasions from playground activities, etc. Nothing too serious from a casual observation, but there was a *bunch* of them. And they were all looking at the newest arrival, who was filling out and signing the fat packet of forms, and who was attached to a dangling, rattling Dive Bomber. Little kids were looking up at their mamas and asking in loud, little kid voices questions like "Mama, what's the matter with that man?" Or, "How do you reckon he did *that*?" Questions everybody was wondering, but only little people would ask out loud. Some asked *real* loud.

On the surface, Bill was ignoring the conversations, but his face was beginning to get pretty red. I had a fleeting notion about trying to inject a little comic relief into the situation by announcing to the crowd that, "He zigged when he should have zagged," or something like that, but since I'm a sensitive, caring person, I decided he might become more uncomfortable if I did. So

168

I didn't. And because of that sensitivity, possibly averted a considerable amount of physical abuse to my own body.

Bill finished the forms and jangled up to the desk to hand them in. Then he jangled back to the waiting area where I had located two adjacent empty chairs. The chairs were on the front row of a lot of rows, which meant that most of the folks were sitting behind us. Which also gave most of them the ability to stare directly into the unblinking eyes of the Dive Bomber. And their interest in the Dive Bomber continued to intensify. Discourteous snickers behind cupped hands, pointing fingers, and loud, creative whispers abounded, deepening the red color of Bill's face and neck.

Bill, being the good salesman he is, understands basic ingredients of human nature, one of which is, "Out of sight, out of mind." So, when he had had a bellyfull of the snickers and whispers, he decided to rectify the situation temporarily by moving to a location which would remove the Dive Bomber from everybody's sight.

There was a Coke machine against the wall of the waiting room, with a little window about shoulder height right next to it. He suggested that we wander over to the machine, have a Coke, and stand there for a while, leaning against the wall so that the Dive Bomber would be hidden from the crowd's view. I agreed. We got a Coke, and he leaned against the wall, with his shoulders against the window sill. To make sure that nobody could see the Dive Bomber from outside, he closed the venetian blinds on the window. He had been right about the loss of interest by everybody when they could no longer see his unwanted appendage. They quieted down and pursued other interests.

From the size of the crowd in the waiting room, I figured we had about an hour's wait before our turn would come up, so I was surprised when the receptionist called out "Jackson" after only about ten minutes. Bill hollered, "Here!" raised his hand with his index finger pointing up, took a giant step toward the receptionist, and almost fell over backward, since a hook on the Dive Bomber had latched onto the venetian blinds' pull cord.

The blinds rattled straight out behind him and the crowd took a new interest in him, and the Dive Bomber persisted, one of its heretofore empty hooks now driven into the tough woven cord. Past the barb. Right above the little bell shaped plastic thing that covers the knot on the end of the cord. And the cord had passed through a couple of the slats near the bottom of the blinds, so between the rattling of the now straight-out blinds and the rattling of the Dive Bomber, considerable racket was taking place. Bill was a little rattled too, evidenced by the fact that he was motionless, standing with his head tilted slightly back toward the straight out blinds. With the giggling from the crowd starting up again. I immediately rushed over to him to offer my services, as I had seemed to have been called on to do all evening. One look at the hooked cord told me that it was not a simple problem.

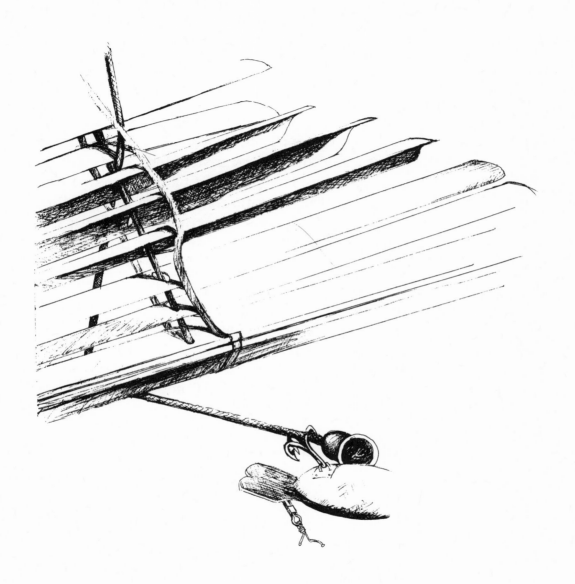

"Bill, you're going to have to take at least one step back so I can have a little slack to work on getting the hook out." I hastened to add, "Out of the cord."

Through clenched teeth he whispered in a hissing sort of way, "Goddammit, just cut the cord off, goddammit, *goddammit*." I whipped out my pocket knife and did as instructed, sawing off the cord just above the hook. The blinds banged back against the window and Bill took off for the receptionist desk to answer the "Jackson" call, the Dive Bomber content for the moment with its new embellishment hanging on the bottom hook and bumping against the back of Bill's neck with every step.

The receptionist looked up at Bill, rolled her eyes toward the ceiling and said, "Mr. Jackson, I was calling for Mr. *Leroy* Jackson. As a matter of fact, there are *several* Jacksons ahead of you. Please be patient."

We went back to the chairs and sat down. For about an hour. Which gave me time to work the Dive Bomber loose from the cord and replace the little plastic thing on the blinds. They looked as good as new.

Bill's turn eventually came and the unimaginative doctor cut the front hooks off my Dive Bomber before he snatched them out of Bill's fat scalp. Snatched them out just like I would have done with the only exception being that he cut the hooks off first. Unnecessarily, I thought. And he did shoot a little novocaine into Bill's fat head before he snatched, but from the screwed up face

Bill made when he was injected with the stinging novocaine, he simply substituted one misery for another.

The doctor put a band-aid on the little rip and wordlessly handed me the Dive Bomber, which I later presented to Bill as a sort of peace offering. Framed. At a big party. With instructions on how to make a weedless Dive Bomber much on the same order as I've given you here. And we're still friends, which tells you what a good man he is.

A word of advice to you here. If you're contemplating making your Dive Bomber weedless, you probably will come out ahead by finding a pair of heavy cutters and just snipping off the front hooks. Or you can do it the way I did. The toughest part of that procedure, however, will likely be to find a partner who'll cooperate.

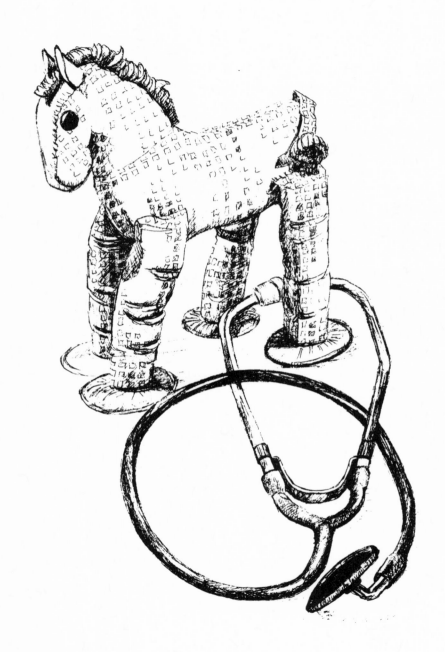

IN WHOM I AM WELL PLEASED

Well, Sport, it's been a very full and interesting month. You've taken in holy matrimony your life's helpmate in the form of the beautiful, redheaded Martha. You've graduated with honors from medical school and been awarded Lieutenant's stripes in Uncle Sam's Navy. And at the time of this writing, you're on your way to your first duty station to begin your work as your brothers' healer.

It absolutely cannot have been twenty-five years since I was calling for your mother on occasion to check your suspicious diapers. (I'll admit to you now that she cheerfully handled that chore and I hated it!) The time warp that has compressed so many stages and events into so short a span seems surreal.

You almost didn't even get started in life. I, in the macho world of the U.S. Army officer corps, had naturally ordered that my firstborn was to be a man child, and that order was never questioned by your mother. We even referred to you as "Sam" while you kicked and turned inside your tiny world of her body, and our excitement grew in concert with your growth. You were scheduled, by all the mysterious ways in which mothers and obstetricians calculate those things, to be born on 25 August, 1962. (I have often been corrected by your mother when I have told people that we were married in June and you were born the following August. She always inserts that I meant August of the following year.)

As luck would have it, I drew Officer of the Day on the night of August 24, which meant that I had to spend the night at battalion headquarters. My first inclination, naturally, was to request that one of my brother officers switch days with me. Any one of them would have gladly done so, but with the unerring logic of a First Lieutenant, I gambled on the old saw that the firstborn is 'most always late, and if you were even one day late, I had a full two weeks before my turn at OD would come up again. So I elected to pull my duty, with the stipulation that your mother spend the night with our most loved friends, Warner and Judy Cole, and that Wayne Cannon, my Battery Commander, also a First Lieutenant and my superior by a full four months date of rank, be on alert should I call him to relieve me.

The telephone rang at about five in the morning of the 25th with Judy on the other end of the line. She advised me in no uncertain terms that I should come at once to deliver your mother to Martin Army Hospital so she could complete a very important delivery of her own. A quick call to Wayne set that part of the plan in motion, and by the time I had pulled on my uniform, his car screeched into the parking lot. I'll never know how he got there so fast, and I'll also never forget the sight of him sailing out into the parking lot holding his shirt in one hand and holding up his fatigue britches with the other, while his unlaced boots flapped with each running step. I ran past him on the way to our little Nash Rambler and hollered "Thanks!" He hollered "Go!" And I went. Too fast, as I recall. Judy handed your mother's little overnight bag over to me. I hurriedly deposited your mother in the car, and raised great billowing clouds of Fort Benning dust on the way to the hospital, while your mother vaguely complained of a blinding headache. I squealed the car on two wheels into the emergency entrance, handed her to the attendant, and parked the car in the lot. I got back to the emergency room in less than two minutes. They had already taken her somewhere else and everyone looked worried. I was directed to a nondescript waiting area and left in isolation to pace, smoke, and wonder. Twenty or so minutes later, I burst back into the emergency room and demanded that I be told where your mother was, or that the hospital would have cause to remember me for a long time. I cringe now at my boorish behavior. The available staff was at that moment frantically using every skill at their disposal to keep you and your mother alive. My threats were evidently convincing enough, however, that a doctor, still in his green baggy scrub suit, came out to give me a progress report. The totally unexpected full-blown case of eclampsia visited on your mother while giving you birth, replete with violent convulsions which started the minute I

177

had delivered her to the emergency room, required massive doses of tranquilizers to quiet her down. These drugs, passed to you through those very passageways which had nurtured you through your formation, made it difficult for the doctors to force you to breathe. I remember writing you off completely in my urgent pleadings to the doctor and frantic prayers to God begging them not to let your mother die. I didn't feel, after the doctor explained the seriousness of eclampsia to me, that I had the right to ask for you both to make it. And I confess to you here that I prayed for her life and not yours. Knowing you as I do now, I reckon you'd approve of that choice. I'll also confess to you that this was the only time in my life that I have felt the helpless, gut-grinding, metallic-tasting emotion of sheer terror. There was nothing I could fight or fend off to protect her or you. Nothing to pound except the walls, which I did. And God had mercy on me. The skill and dedication of that group of military doctors and nurses who stayed with you and your mother through the next three days of your fragile existence makes it appropriate somehow that your first assignment be in a military hospital. And I hope that you attain the level of magnificence that those people showed. I can never repay them.

But you made it! You *both* made it! Praise be to God! *You both made it!*

The growing up of both of us during this twenty-five years has been fun and educating and worrisome and rewarding for me. Mostly fun and educating and rewarding. The metamorphosis from the chubby, dimpled, bald baby through the stocky, husky, tow head to the clumsy, opinionated adolescent, then to the young adult grown to the stature where you had to nod your head forward to look your old man in the eye, encompasses an avalanche of memories, each of which gives rise to miniavalanches of more. Even the diaper changing.

One of your first accomplishments I can remember was the taking advantage of the inexperience your mother and I had with little bitty boys peeing straight up with considerable force at the critical moment of the diaper changing. After the wet diaper had been removed, the bottom washed and powdered, and the new diaper placed underneath and ready to be pinned, like a miniature (*real* miniature) spitting cobra, the little tallywhacker always aimed for the eyes. And your accuracy was uncanny. Real or imaginary, I usually detected a smirk which silently said "GOTCHA!" Suited me. I admired the marksmanship. *My* son had *velocity*! And shot *straight*!

You weren't much to look at in the first month. Both of your grandmothers naturally remarked over and over about what a pretty baby you were. I kept peering at you closer time and time again to see if they were able to observe something I was over-looking. Scrawny, wrinkled, absolutely bald, eyes crossing and uncrossing, uncoordinated, loudly demanding, and always ammonia-reeking wet. I considered those things liabilities, but I learned real quick not to voice my opinion about them to your mother or grandmothers. I just kept the faith that one day you

179

would assume a more human form. And, of course, you did. My concern diminished and pride increased with each pound gained and each wrinkle lost. Pretty soon, I was able to offer to friends and acquaintances without reservation that you belonged to me and your mother. They usually did the talking. "Stocky little devil, isn't he?" or "Boy, he doesn't miss a thing. Look at the way he's sizing me up!" I wouldn't say much. Just grinned inside. Unless, of course, they missed something. Then I'd fill in the gaps they had missed. Ad nauseam, I now suppose.

Well, you learned to laugh and to crawl and to walk. You cut all of your teeth and you learned the language. Just like any other normal kid. But to your mother and me, each accomplishment was an adventure and we marveled at them. It was fun to watch.

The memories get a little murky for the period of tiny babyhood until you reached about three years' age, when distinct traits began to emerge. Curious, quick-witted, verbose, obstinate, persuasive. All of these adjectives conjure up tales.

There was at the time a bubble bath marketed under the name "Soaky". It came in plastic bottles molded in the shape of Mickey Mouse or Pluto or some such. I made the mistake of taking a Soaky bath with you one time, and for a period, you invited me to join you at each bath time, and my excuses for demurring began to run out. One specific time I remember, you issued your standard request for me to take a Soaky bath with you and I once again found a reason to decline. Then the persuasive trait surfaced. "But, Daddy," you persisted, holding a bottle out for my inspection, "this is a brand new bottle of Soaky in a Sylvester Cat bottle. It hasn't even been opened yet." It was a sales pitch, pure and simple, and since I was a peddler myself, it pleased me. I said, "Boy, here I am, an IBM salesman, a member of one of the most accomplished sales forces in the world, and you're trying to sell *me*?" I remember the puzzled look your face took on for a moment, then you informed me, "Naw, Daddy. I don't want to *sell* you. I want to *keep* you!" As I recall, we took the Soaky bath.

You seemed to wonder at the most common things. The pattern was, you'd focus intently on an object, and I could almost hear the wheels turning. I'd usually try and vacate the premises before the inevitable "Why" question would impale me.

We'd been through the old standard "Why is the grass green?" and "Why is the sky blue?" stuff, and I handled them pretty well because I knew they were coming and had prepared pretty pat answers. The "Why is concrete so hard?" or "Is steel harder than iron? Why?" types were what used to give me fits. You'd stare at a tree swaying in the breeze, for example, and if I stuck around I'd get, "Daddy, does the wind start somewhere or does it just keep going forever?"

One night I came home late from work and arrived while you were taking a bath. I looked in on you and we began chatting about various three-year-old topics. Suddenly you stopped talking, began staring at the water, and the wheels started whirring again. I almost made it to the door.

"Daddy!!"

I slowly turned and took a deep breath, waiting for the quiz.

"Why can't 'cha dig a hole in water?"

Try explaining *that* to a three year old. I stumbled through the three types of matter, and when I got to the liquids assuming the shape of their container, you were lost, but nodded as if you understood it anyway. I realized in that moment that I was an absolute failure as a father for not being able to expound in understandable, perfectly simple, three-year-old logic on advanced physics, nuclear science and anthropology ("Why do dogs have four legs and we only have two?") What to do? How the hell do I correct this deficiency?

At that very instant the phone rang. Fellow was selling encyclopedia sets and wanted to set up an appointment. I told him that an appointment would not be necessary, since I wanted to see him right then. He said, "Sir, it's eight P.M. Could we perhaps schedule the appointment for tomorrow?" I asked whether a contract signed at night was valid, and when he answered in the affirmative, I suggested that perhaps he might better get his ass over here if he wanted to sell me one of those encyclopedias. Which he did. I bought everything he had to offer including the encyclopedia set, the Book of Knowledge set, the Book of Science set, some other big book, and enough bookcases to house the whole shooting match.

The transaction took about five minutes, with the only real decision being whether I wanted the color of the encyclopedia covers to be maroon or blue. Since I didn't allow anything maroon in my house, I chose blue.

I'm sure that the salesman, a nice little oriental fellow, left our house shaking his head and he probably used that call as a war story in later sales seminars.

Your mother caught her share of your questions too, of course, but she used the phrase "That's just the way God made it" a lot. Her trials seemed to take a little different twist.

You loved to go to the zoo, and she took you there often. One day your interest shifted from the lions and tigers to, of all things, a strutting old tom turkey. The big old tom had spread his tail feathers and bowed out his wings, and was putting on a show. Several other people were gathered around watching his performance. He turned his backside to you and the rest of the crowd, and his rectum began to first extrude and then pucker back up in a series of rapid movements, as a tom turkey will often do in the strut. Your clear, high pitched voice rang out, obviously thrilled, and with volume enough for all around to hear, "Mama, look! That turkey likes me!"

"What makes you say that, Jimmy?", she whispered, knowing immediately that she shouldn't have posed the question.

"He's *winkin'* at me!"

She said something spectacular like "Unh-hunh," and took your hand and headed off to look at the bears, leaving the laughing crowd watching you waving good-bye to the friendly turkey.

It wasn't all hearts and flowers, of course. The experience of raising young'uns has created a few memories I'd just as soon forget. Like your allergy test when you were about age seven. You'd been snuffling and snorting enough to raise suspicions in your mother's mind that allergies were present, and at the appointed time, you and I headed to the clinic to let the experts hopefully dispel that motherly concern. No problem. The doctor had told us that the test consisted of a few scratches to the skin of the back, dispensing a drop of some substances on the scratches, and observing the reactions to determine whether allergies existed. You and I figured we'd get that over with in a couple of minutes and be off again in a jiffy.

The nurse cheerfully instructed you to remove your shirt and lie face down on the table so that she could make a few "little cat scratches" and solve any mysteries which might exist. You, face down, were relaxed about the proceedings, and I, watching, was caught up in the scientific aspects of the event. Until the "little cat scratching" started. She took a pin and started the systematic creation of neat rows of scratches. The first one, while it drew the blood it was supposed to, wasn't too bad on either of us. Nor was the second, or third, or fourth. At about the dozenth, when I was sure she was near the end, you reached up to the head of the table and gripped it with both hands. Sweat started popping out all over you, and still she scratched. You gripped harder, making no sound, and still she scratched. I gripped the edge of the tall stool I was sitting on, and still she scratched. I suggested to the nurse that she was rapidly running out of back surface to scratch on and if she didn't get through pretty soon, maybe she could put a few of those damned scratches on me. Fortunately for all of us, she finished at that moment, or I don't think I would have made it. Three things I remember about that procedure...the neat rows of bloody scratches on my son's back, the fact that my sweaty, tense, hurting little boy had made no sound, and my anger at that seemingly unfeeling nurse. When the ordeal was over, and the allergies had been identified, you slipped back into your shirt and we sailed out of the office, laughing and joking about the whole happening. Oh, yeah. And the fourth thing was that your shirt was dry, and mine was soaking wet.

Then there was THE SPANKING shortly thereafter. I don't remember really spanking you but once, and the memory of it still rankles. We'd been on a trip to somewhere and were returning home, having been on the road almost all day, and all of us were tired and restless. You and your little sister were on the back seat of the car and you were regularly pestering her to tears. Consoling words of promise that we'd soon be home and finally, threats had been passed from both sides of the front seat to you to cease and desist or else. My words were, "If it happens one more time, when we get home...." Every parent can identify with the scenario. Well, of course, it happened one more time, and the die was unavoidably cast. We pulled into our driveway, unloaded, and I directed you to the bathroom. I folded the seat down on the toilet, sat down, and very pompously asked you if you remembered why we were there. You didn't say anything. Just nodded. I felt like I was participating in an execution. You were ordered to drop your pants, which you did, and I folded you across my lap, bare bottom up. The spanking was applied in a vigorous flurry of barehanded slaps until a sob which I can still hear was obtained. God dammit! I still hate the sound of that sob. Then we headed our separate ways in a hurry, your bottom burning and my stomach in a bile-filled knot. Years earlier, my papa had given me the old, "This is going to hurt me more than it does you," and I never believed him until that day.

There's not room here to go into all of the dove, quail, duck, and deer hunts, or the fishing trips we made beginning as soon as you were able to walk for a half-mile dragging a plastic gun. And while there were plenty of them, I wish now that there had been more. Each one of them could be a story in itself, and I strain against launching off into an epic describing them. Maybe later.

I guess I wasn't too fond of giving you lectures or imparting sage, formal, everlasting advice because I wasn't always sure that I had all the right answers. You began to get a glimmer of my predicament one night when you were sixteen and announced to your mother and me that you had been invited to a party to be held at one of our friends' cabins in the country, and asked to use the car. I knew that this particular event was geared to the older kids of college age, and I suggested that your going might not be such a good idea. The debate started, heated up, and should an outsider have been listening, he probably would have been under the impression that your very psyche was in danger of impairment should you not be allowed to go. The decision stood, however, and when you realized that, you started toward your room, stopped, slowly turned around and said, "Does it occur to you that you might possibly be wrong about this?" I admitted that there was that possibility. "But," I said, "you will just have to be patient with me. You see, I've never raised a sixteen year old before, just like you have never been sixteen before. So if you'll hang in there with me, I'll hang in there with you, and between us, mistakes and all, we'll muddle through this thing together." And we did. Through the high school days culminating in your emerging Salutatorian, college days, graduating Magna Cum Laude, and the aforementioned honors at med school. And I enjoyed it.

Now you're headed out in your own direction, wherever that adventure might lead. I'll follow that journey with a tad more than passing interest, and I'll try and be here if you need me.

So, go get 'em, Doc. The world is a hell of a good place, and your charge is to make it better, as I know you will. Maybe one day I'll have the courage to voice something I've felt for a long time to the present world and to those who will follow. I've introduced you to a lot of individuals and groups over the years. And I've wanted to use the words which were used by another Father, but were never used by me because they could have been interpreted in an erroneous, sacrilegious way. Nevertheless, I can identify with the love and pride and satisfaction expressed by the simple, eloquent introduction etched in the third chapter of St. Matthew, which begins, "This is my beloved son...."